FOLLOWING THE FULHAM
– THE PREMIERSHIP YEARS

FOLLOWING THE FULHAM
– THE PREMIERSHIP YEARS

PETER THOMSON

ASHWATER
PRESS

First published in October 2008

Copyright © Peter Thomson 2008

Designed and published for Peter Thomson by
Ashwater Press
68 Tranmere Road, Whitton, Twickenham, Middlesex, TW2 7JB
www.ashwaterpress.co.uk

Printed by Ian Allan Printing, Hersham, Surrey

ISBN 978-0-9548938-9-7

PROLOGUE

IN 2002 Harris and Fullbrook published *The Premiership Diary* – 224 pages devoted to a single Fulham season.

I am attempting to catch seven seasons in 140 pages. Thus please find not *2001–2008 The Premiership Diaries* but more *Random Recollections of our Premiership Years to Date*. You may have instant and total recall of all the matches from those years but I have forgotten some and I wish I could forget others. You may consider my recollections partial in another sense, partial as in 'unbalanced and lacking in proper objectivity'. Guilty as charged, guilty and unashamed, because impartiality is for referees and / or couch potatoes.

Having followed the Fulham for 57 seasons, I claim the right to a little bias. My wife describes me as lacking gravitas. Guilty again, but Ernie Clay and David Bulstrode didn't respond to gravitas. It took partiality, obstinate partiality, to keep the faith then. Powered by passion is the *Toofif* boast and powered by passion is what characterised Fulham 2000. This plaque was placed in 1999 before we reached the Premiership and many of these random recollections touch on people and places before August 2001.

Fulham Football Club and Craven Cottage are about much more than a particular season or a particular division. In 1986–87 we were fighting more than relegation and in 1997 we were cele-brating more than promotion. There have been some great days in these Premiership years. We all have the official videos—'Worth the Wait' from the Chelsea, Arsenal and Portsmouth matches. Worth the wait they were but even worthier of the wait was the Bolton fixture of August 2004. That was worth waiting for and worth fighting for, that was BTTC, that was 'Back to the Cottage', that was home again, home again, jiggety-jog. Simply the best was that return to the gloriously refurbished Cottage. Thank you, Chairman Mo!

The Crystal Palace fixture of January 2005 was an extraordinary match. Extraordinary not because we won 3–1 after a long run of defeats but because we were honouring Mary Doughty. Mary was partial, partial to Fulham, partial for Fulham—powered by passion was Mary.

With a little bit of luck (and a lot of help from Ashwater Press) these random recollections should be available at the Hammersmith End around the time of the Maestro's birthday. Johnny Haynes did not play in the Premiership but he was part of these Premiership years. The honours system somehow forgot him but the Stevenage Road became him. He delighted in the architecture of Archibald Leitch and it is entirely appropriate that Leitch refurbished should be renamed in his honour.

The Johnny Haynes Stand contains J block. Not a place for the impartial that J block. Several of those powered by passion linger there. Dennis Turner is the historian's historian, Dennis Turner is the master craftsmen and the embodiment of gravitas, but even he is partial to the spirit (and spirits) of J block. These random recollections of the Premiership years have been inspired by many of those who linger on long after the final whistle. Some of them are Premiership players, some of them are Premiership supporters but all of them are followers of the Fulham, partial and powered by passion.

Over to Chaucer (as concise and as cogent as Dennis Turner): *amor vincit omnia.*

Now read on…

CONTENTS

OPENING UP and CLOSING DOWN
BLACK AND WHITE ARMY?
ACKNOWLEDGEMENTS

ABSENT FRIENDS 38
ACME THE THUNDERER 42
ALL THE GOODIES IN THE
 COTTAGE PIE 44
AND SO TO BED 142
AROUND THE GROUNDS 97
AS OTHERS SEE US 71
BACK HOME – AUGUST 2004 48
BEYOND OUR KEN or OVER TO
 ORMONDROYD 108
BLUE IS THE COLOUR 124
CAN WE PLAY YOU EVERY
 WEEK? 35
CC 68
CENTURY OF TIGERS, A 131
CHOIR POWER 105
CLOSE TO HOME 92
COMMUNITY SERVICE 126
CONTINUITY MAN 112
CRICKET, LOVELY CRICKET 65
DEAR BILL 103
DERBY DAYS AND DERBY
 NIGHTS 86
DUE NORTH? DUE SOUTH? 137
FOLLOWING THE FULHAM INTO
 EUROPE 40
FROM OUR OWN
 CORRESPONDENT 28
FROM THE GREEN POLE,
 2001–2008 47
FULHAM FAMILY IN HAMBURG . . . 95
FULHAM'S PREMIERSHIP XI 115
GOING, GOING, GONE 88
GOLDEN GIRLS 72

HAPPY DAYS 123
HAPPY HOUR 18
HEARTS AND MINDS 26
HOUSE THAT JACK BUILT, THE 89
KEEPING THE FAITH 119
LARKIN ABOUT IN HULL 129
LG THE EMAIL 61
LOOKING GOOD 51
MEANWHILE IN MORTLAKE 62
MY FAVOURITE GRAFFITI 70
NOT ONLY BUT ALSO 121
ON THE ONE HAND 114
ONE OF US 117
ONLY THE LONELY? 80
PARADISE REGAINED 15
POWERED BY PASSION 84
SAMMY – 10th JULY 2008 99
SIMPLY THE BEST 33
SPONSORS PAST AND SPONSORS
 PRESENT 59
STORM IN A D CUP 50
TALES FROM THE RIVERBANK . . . 100
THAT WAS THE TEAM 76
THEN AND NOW 64
ULHAM, ULHAM, WHAT'S THE
 SCORE? 135
WE ARE SURVIVORS 46
WHAT A DIFFERENCE A WEEK
 MAKES or "A LIFE IN THE
 DAY OF..." 132
WHAT WE WANT IS WATNEY'S 22
WHERE WERE YOU 30
WORSE THAN THE YEOVIL 56
YOU'RE HAVING A LAUGH! 78

OPENING UP and CLOSING DOWN

BACK IN THE 1950s, while Johnny Haynes was honing his skills under Bedford Jezzard, I was learning the historian's craft under Walter Ullmann.

Professor Ullmann advocated the detailed study of what happened, when, where and how it happened – "wie es eigentlich gewesen, nicht wahr?"

Fulham has enjoyed a rich tradition of such Ullmannic history. Turner, White, Plumb, Ferguson and Coton have produced magisterial and definitive accounts of Fulham in general and Haynes in particular.

Such scholarship is beyond me and (as a retired academic) I lean more and more towards the *Toofif* school of history. Both editions of *Following the Fulham* sold out, so there are some fans looking for fantasy as well as fact.

A quorum of such fans must have been at Fratton Park this May because after the game I was asked again and again: "Where is the next volume of *Following the Fulham*?" Well here it is, but perhaps not quite as before.

I had not come across David Peace in 2001. Cloughie I knew but not *The Damned United*. Peace hammers home repetition and reiteration. "Repetition, repetition. By Elland Road I sat down and wept. DUFC." I echo this with "By Loftus Road I sat down and wept. BTTC, BTTC." Peace hammers on: "Repetition, repetition. By Elland Road I sat down and wept. DUFC." This

time my answer is: "Back at Stevenage Road, back at the Hammersmith End, back by the riverside I stood up and cheered. FFC, FFC, FFC!"

David Peace concentrates on just 44 days while I rattle around eight years but we both depend heavily on the riches of earlier seasons. Such random recollections can never replace the facts and the footnotes but they might just add some colour to these Premiership years. The fears and tears of 1951–1996 intrude here and there because all our yesterdays make us what we are today – survivors, warts

FULHAM FOOTBALL AND ATHLETIC Co. Ltd.

Registered Office: Craven Cottage, Stevenage Road, Fulham, S.W.6

Directors—T. TRINDER (Chairman), N. A. D'AMATO (Vice-Chairman),
R. A. DEAN, J. G. WALSH, C. B. DEAN.
Secretary and General Manager—F. R. OSBORNE.

Medical Officer—Dr. W. R. D. WIGGINS, M.R.C.S., D.A., R.C.P. and S. (England)
Team Manager—B. JEZZARD. **Trainer**—F. PENN.
Telephone—RENOWN 5621. **Telegrams**—" FULHAMISH, LONDON, S.W.6."

Saturday, 12th November, 1960 Kick off 2.30 p.m.

INSIDE THE COTTAGE

and all survivors. Fulhamish very. Yesterday's telegram is our tomorrow and tomorrow. In the beginning was the word and the word was Fulhamish.

CLOSING DOWN

Last season our away form was deeply dire and confirmed our place in the relegation zone. The morticians had gathered around Freddie Fulham's slab and at half-time against Man City (when we were two goals down and 'relegated') the coins were being placed on Freddie's eyelids.

Time for a Freddie Fulhamish moment – get up, wake up and win. Win again away at Reading and pop down to Pompey. Spoil the party for the cup finalists. Have a bit of fun in the sun. Still relegated at half-time and at three-quarter-time, but we score the late, late goal and survive on goal difference. Away wins are nil for most of the season, then we have three on the trot. Revival and survival the hard way. Freddie Fulham says: "The impossible takes longer with FFC."

Just ask Ray Lewington about Fulhamish. Here a win, there a win, everywhere a win, a win for our Manager of the Month in the March of 1989, so let's celebrate in style at Chester. Seven Up? Why not? Seven up to Chester? Why not indeed? Because it's Fulham 0 (as in nil) Chester 7 (as in seven). Seventh heaven for them and a blush or two for us.

Come the following Saturday the Manager of the Month duly received his magnum of champagne at Craven Cottage; our very own Sammy the steward was on parade and joined the official presentation party before solemnly handing his can of Seven Up to Ray Lewington. A perfect touch of the *Toofifs*, for April Fool's Day some twenty years ago.

This August we are at it again. Playing the beautiful game beautifully for twenty minutes up at Hull we then fall asleep, fall apart and lose a winnable fixture. Bring on the Arsenal, past masters and pass masters who are then out-passed and outclassed by FFC for 70 minutes. There is, of course, still time for the team to take a nap before the final whistle, still ample time for a dozen Arsenal free kicks and corners. Nerves must be shredded before the win is won.

13th September 2008. Enter the Trotters far right – dressed in Australian rugby colours and imitating Australian rugby forwards in their robust muscularity. Enter Roy's boys left – and deft. Far too deft for Bolton, two up and strolling. Even the Riverside mutes are calling for three or four or more, but just in case we should think we are as good as we look we let them score and press the panic button. Chaos and confusion to cure our complacency.

Thus league form is erratic but entertaining. What of the Carling Cup and the softly softly route to Wembley? Home to relegated Leicester. Easy win? Early goal and a comfortable first half. Seconds out, second half. Leicester score once, Leicester score twice. We are playing badly and even Jimmy Bullard is having an off off night. Typical Fulham – early exit badly mauled by lower league lions (Leyton Orient, Bristol Rovers). "Premiership? You're having a larf!"

Jimmy Bullard unamused by such taunts charges towards the Hammersmith End and unleashes a thunderbolt. 2–2 and we are looking at extra time/penalties. We have lost on penalties to Leicester – ask CC. Injury time is upon us and Captain Murphy smacks the ball against a Leicester shin. Deliciously cruel deflection for an own goal. 3–2 and final whistle. Talk about lucky, lucky Fulham. Well, talk about lucky, lucky Fulham until you hear that in the next round of the Carling Cup we are away to… Burnley. Even JT and the dream team couldn't win at Turf Moor. Serves us right for thinking that life could ever be plain sailing down by the riverside.

13th September 2008. Phone call from Ashwater Press. "That's it. Time is up. No more words." Oh, you lucky people!

No more words? Perhaps just one last local acronym: *FTID*.

Peter Thomson, Mortlake, September 2008.

BLACK AND WHITE ARMY?

HARDLY AN ARMY, just a dozen Fulhamish foot soldiers. Humble infantry-men who have served on all the Premiership campaigns. Most of this old guard go back to 1975 and the long march to Wembley. It is possible to name names and date dates by consulting our visitors' book. Sheila hosted a promotion party in May 2001 and each guest indicated his/her first season with FFC.

There are the veterans, those who remember Haynes, Cohen, Callaghan and Cook. Together they sang "Jimmy Conway on the wing!" Together they watched in disbelief as the Maestro's men slipped down the divisions in 1968 and 1969. They are Arundel Roger, Brian Gee, Derek Humphris, David the lawyer, Jason the artist and Derek the framer.

Then there are the four stalwarts from 1983, survivors from the Ivor era when we almost managed a double promotion. The Quayles (Alan and Karen) plus our corporals of horse Steven and Andy – cavalry then but trainspotters now kindly assisting with matchday travel.

In 1998 we enlisted Björn and thus set up a base camp in Hamburg, little thinking that we would ever take part in continental campaigns. Yet in 2002 over there we were. Above you see those who met up with Björn in Berlin. Intertoto done and won. Croatia conquered – UEFA, UEFA! Following the Fulham into Europe.

In addition there are Petes aplenty. From 1951 there is PFT; in the Riverside dug-out there is Pete the stretcher bearer; from Norwich there is Pete the golfer. Most recent Pete is the photographer from Edinburgh who documented our visit to Fratton Park.

Some campaigns were more Tolstoy tours than Thomson holidays. Through the ice and snow to Lincoln in December 1995. Lincoln 4 Fulham 0. Then for the retreat from Moscow – more ice, more snow. Are we downhearted, little black and white army? Yes and no. Corporal Jones cheers the troops with the prospect of sunny Torquay where surely we will turn things around. We did. We lost again and moved into 91st position, so convenient for the Conference. Almost the Conference, but not quite the Conference for the black and white army.

Instead of Crawley and Woking we face Sochaux and Bologna. More balmy army than barmy army in Bologna – Inamoto for the Intertoto. Fulham pensioners are we, soldiering on. We are the walking wounded of the Premiership. Soldiering on with a bit of a song: "Who put the ball in the Pompey net? Murphy! Murphy!"

ACKNOWLEDGEMENTS

Every picture tells a story. There are many pictures here and lots of stories. Some of the pictures come from the Coton archive, and the stories are all the better for Ken's visual aids. Some of the stories were inspired by the photographs of Ken and the images of Ormondroyd – all were processed at Ashwater Press. As editor, Ken has improved the text but the faults/follies/fantasies are mine. Without Ken, *The Premiership Years* would have been less easy on the eye and much less fun to write.

Dennis Turner, Alex White and Martin Plumb have provided the very best of reference books on our club. All followers of the Fulham are indebted to them – their writings have sustained us through tricky days in exile at Loftus Road. David Lloyd and the *Toofif* team have asked the right questions throughout these Premiership years. The chapter on page 84 is dedicated to them.

The chairman, directors and officers of FFC have provided me with 57 years worth of material, match magazines and a second home. I gratefully acknowledge the club in the production of this book.

My thanks go to all those friends, fans and family members who have contributed anecdotes – and more – to these reminiscences. In particular Derek Humphris and David Roodyn – Derek for proofreading and guidance home and away (1975–2008), David for his essay *We Are Survivors* and for many another wise word (1968–2008).

All followers of Fulham and fellow travellers have helped me to survive and to celebrate 1951–2008. Much as I have enjoyed the years 2001–2008 (particularly the Intertoto/UEFA tour) the real joy has been in surviving and celebrating with other followers of the Fulham – especially Sheila. When I came a-courting in August 1980 (Fulham 0 Hull 0, crowd 4,592) Sheila may not have realised quite what was involved in following the Fulham. The learning curve, the ups and downs (particularly the downs and downs of 1986–1996) must have tested her patience and marriage vows. There were evening games when Concorde flying above the Cottage was the most exciting moment in the match. There were away days at Derby, Swansea and Torquay when the weather was grim and the results grimmer, but Sheila was there for Fulham and there for me.

ILLUSTRATIONS

Many illustrations are from the author's archive. Others – which are gratefully acknowledged – are by Ken Coton, Ormondroyd and numerous fans and friends. If any copyright has been unwittingly infringed, please contact the author.

For Sheila.

PARADISE REGAINED

"PARADISE REGAINED" were the last two words of *Following The Fulham* and they were written in August 2001 on the eve of our return to the top table after an absence of 33 years. At the time "Paradise regained!" but it probably should have been "Paradise regained?" Given the style with which Tigana's team had won promotion we were not overanxious about survival in the Premiership. Saha's spectacular goals up at Old Trafford proved that we could compete (and entertain) at the highest level.

A solid performance at home to Sunderland suggested that we could cope with bread and butter opposition. Barry Hayles scored the first goal and Saha the second. After the match Hayles was quick to stress the importance of the crowd. "I can't remember a better atmosphere at the Cottage." Worth waiting for and worth relishing. So far so good on the pitch but paradise regained?

The question mark was there because we did not know what was to be done about Craven Cottage. The open terraces had to go. Fulham could not retain standing room at the Hammersmith and Putney ends. Where were we to play while the all-seater stadium was constructed? How much of the old Fulham would remain after modernisation? The Cottage itself was scheduled for demolition. Paradise regained but at what cost?

Such doubts were on hold for the last week of September as we looked forward to the fixture of fixtures – Chelsea back at the Cottage. Memories of another September in 1975 (Fulham 2 Chelsea 0) or of Ivor's hat trick in 1983 but most especially of Good Friday 1977 and October 1979 when bottom of the table Fulham beat top of the table Chelsea.

And so to 30th September 2001. Come the day it was not a particularly distinguished game. Chelsea's manager praised Fulham for playing "champagne football" but after all the anticipation the champagne tasted flat. Honours even at 1–1 (Hasselbaink for Chelsea, Hayles for Fulham).

Tigana had secured 14 away wins to take the Division One title but it was November before we gained our first Premiership victory away from Craven Cottage – West Ham 0 Fulham 2 (Legwinski and Malbranque).

Remember, remember the 17th of November. November was an important month for Fulham in general and for this Fulham family in particular. The lawyers were busy in the High Court arguing over the plans for a 30,000-seater stadium and at the Ashwater Press the porters were unloading the first thousand copies of *Following the Fulham*. Mr Justice Collins would give his judgement

Winning striker, losing streaker. (Hayles on target.)

after Christmas but the fans would assess *Following the Fulham* at the Newcastle match. Luckily it was a terrific game with Saha in fine form and a Shearer penalty saved by Edwin van der Sar (plus a streaker).

The feel-good factor after a 3–1 win certainly helped sales of *Following the Fulham* but any personal euphoria was offset by the team's fragility away from Craven Cottage. Spurs beat us 4–0 at White Hart Lane. It could have been even worse at Highbury had Wenger not removed Henry with the Arsenal 4–1 ahead. Come 24th March, Spurs completed the double with a 2–0 win at the Cottage and Fulham had lost six consecutive league matches. Premiership panic. Paradise at risk.

Standing in the snow at Highbury I met up with Steve Magee. A dedicated follower of Fulham and sometime groundsman at the Cottage, Steve had put together an unbroken sequence of 730 games home and away so there was much to remember but we were too cold and too dispirited to do more than shake hands, shake heads and point to the relegation zone.

Fulham's poor run in the Premiership was partially disguised by success in the FA Cup. Defeating lower division opponents such as Wycombe, York, Walsall and West Bromwich Albion took us through to the semi-final for the first time since 1975 and provided one more opportunity to have a go at Chelsea. The chairman generously subsidised the trains and coaches to Villa Park but it was a poor game. A nothing goal from which we failed to recover, then a long, long wait for our trains and a long, long limp home.

For me the most memorable part of the cup run was the visit to York in January. With their ground at risk and facing a major financial crisis, York's

situation was as grim as that of Fulham in 1987. There was a warm welcome for the Fulham fans and delight at the chairman's donation of the £50,000 match fee to the York City Trust Fund. An entertaining game with good goals from Steed and Marlet made up for some of the Premiership grind.

Premiership grind? Hardly the paradise regained which had been so keenly anticipated in the summer of 2001. All made worse when Dennis Turner and I were recruited to a Fulham think tank hosted by Juliet Slot. The club had decided to take advice on the disposal of assets ahead of redevelopment. Fair enough to sell turf to fans but a limited edition of 800 bricks from the soon-to-be-demolished Cottage? Alarm bells off the pitch in addition to the threat of relegation.

Victory at Elland Road lifted the gloom (thanks Steed) and set up the crunch game with Bolton on the Tuesday evening. The last floodlit game to be played at the old Craven Cottage and a performance to savour. Goldbaek proved the man of the match. His bouncing bomb provided the first goal and he assisted Marlet to the second. Hayles made sure of victory with the third goal and the fans could relax at last assured of Premiership safety. Rapture for some. Muted applause from others as the High Court appeals process meant that Fulham's Premiership football would be at Loftus Road for two seasons rather than one.

"Fulham fans watched the final game at the old Craven Cottage with a sense of relief" – Harry Harris in his *Premiership Diary*. Relief at avoiding relegation but many other emotions too. Delight at the sight of Mr Adams, now the Leicester manager, but forever associated with his contribution to Fulham's promotion from the fourth division. Pride when the veterans paraded before the match – the Maestro and Tosh, Mullers and Morgs, George Cohen and Ivor. Frustration that the football did not match the occasion. Sorrow at the realisation that it would be two years or more before we would again watch football beside the river.

Long after the final whistle fans lingered on remembering other games and other players. Ghosts. Ghosts and gremlins. The gremlins of anxiety about the future of the ground. The season which had begun with such confidence had ended Miltonian and Fulhamish. More *Paradise Lost* than *Paradise Regained*?

The certainty of August 2001 had given way to the uncertainty of April 2002. All newly promoted teams should read the government health warning: "To Purgatory fire thou comest at last!"

We did not read the small print. We thought it was all about Paradise regained but it soon proved otherwise. We were "lost in a sort of purgatory."

Perhaps *Following The Fulham – The Premiership Years* should have the sub-title "Feel the flames."

HAPPY HOUR

THE HOUR OR so when you meet up with your fellow followers of the Fulham. Somehow it is going to be all right this time. Despite recent form you sense that Arsenal or Chelsea or Liverpool or Man Utd are vulnerable. Derek has heard that their main man is carrying an injury, Steven reckons that their keeper has been tapped up by the Italians, Alan's friends at the Oval know Smith who used to coach their manager. Karen listens and smiles. By the time we leave Becky and The Bricklayer's, we are quietly confident (not just the Dutch courage of Timothy Taylor's fine ales). We all enjoy the river views and the stroll through Bishop's Park. Happy hour, happy hours before kick-off. Less joy at 5.50pm in these Premiership years, relegation avoidance is achieved more by earnest application than by flow and flair. Even when we win it is received with a sigh of relief rather than celebrated with that careless rapture which characterised the fixtures of 1999 and 2001.

HAPPIER HOUR / HOURS

Away days offer extra time, time added on and inevitably injury time (that cup semi-final at Villa Park), but let's be positive about following the Fulham in the Premiership years.

The golden age of steam (Doughty days and Doughty nights) coincided with Ken's golden years as Fulham's photographer and prime time with Haynes and Hill, Lawler, Langley and Leggat, Cohen and co. Away days then featured milk trains via Crewe when warm waiting rooms welcomed us at 2am. Top man Topley did us proud in 1997. Silver service from Chris as we clocked up the miles and the away wins.

The golden age of steam – and a golden age when supporters could chat with players on train journeys to and from matches. Here Ian Seymour listens to fans following a postponed match at Preston in November 1968.

A dozen such victories equals 36 points (compare and contrast with one away win a season in 2005–06 and 2006–07). The season of seasons was 2001 with 14 away wins. Best ever in terms of results but Topley tours were at risk. Dr Beeching did for good old British Rail; some nameless / faceless official fragmented the networks just as Chairman Mo, KK and JT were restoring FFC.

True there were some happy hours on trains to Chesterfield. Selecting our best-ever XI (difficult choosing between Macedo and Peyton in goal), selecting our worst-ever XI (easy – up front John Watson, with Jim Hicks an automatic choice as central defenceless). Crossword puzzles at the *Toofif* table with assists from Chris Guard.

Sudoku was probably invented in 2001 to celebrate our arrival in the Premiership. Sheila is 'difficult', 'challenging', 'fiendish' and 'killer'. I prefer to sit at the trivial pursuits table with Derek. We have selected Fulham's best-ever Premiership XI. Easy in goal – VDS, and easy up front – Saha; but what about the midfield? Is there a place for Lee Clark? Time to choose Fulham's worst-ever Premiership XI. Jensen N as most disappointing international defender, Elrich as consistently poor midfielder, the Korean so good for Reading so poor for us. And as for Baird? What was wrong with Liam? Why no Volz under Sanchez? Good heavens, are we at Ipswich, Norwich, Reading, Southampton, Portsmouth already? One happy hour gone but quick, quick and into a CAMRA approved pub for another happy hour.

Credit Steven with transport arrangements for Premiership fixtures. He is most expert in detours and discounts. Doughty / Topley memorial medals for Steve – his first awarded for distinguished service throughout these Premiership years. Where would we have been without him? Even when the rails melted at Windsor he got us to Livingston via Waverley in time for a happy hour with their manager, Jolly Jim Leishman. Steven's second medal is for gallantry. He attended every away game in 2006–07. Just the one win. How many happy hours that season as the train took the strain and the pain?

HAPPIEST HOUR

That hour with the fixture list in June 2001. That hour when the 33 years of exile were officially over. Fulham must be back because it says so here in black and white. Yes, black and white for the black and whites. Old Trafford in August, Anfield in December, Highbury in February, Stamford Bridge in March.

"Bliss was it in that dawn to be alive, but to be Fulham was very heaven." Bliss indeed for one happy hour but then as dates are entered in diaries the sudden realisation that my Fulham born and bred son and heir Ian has arranged his wedding for August 18th when we are away to Man Utd. Club versus country, family versus FFC. Not such a happy hour of ringing around and making excuses, listening to chants of "Call yourself a Fulham fan!"

Fear not, there may yet be a solution to this conflict of interests. Perhaps Jonathan (Undertaker) Sim can sort it out at Sky. Indeed he can. Wedding as planned on the Saturday, Premiership debut moved to the Sunday.

Fast forward from 2001 to 2008. Just when I think things couldn't get any worse on the field (soccer with Sanchez, hoof it up and hash it up), it is all falling apart off the field. Medical matters. Hospital appointments. Shadows on lungs according to the x-rays. Loss of weight and loss of sleep. Blame the football team, blame the medical team.

Time for me to escape from the Premiership. Time to escape from England. Off to Africa on a safari to Khayelitsha. The Homestead hostel there has long been a distant outpost

Premiership wedding for Ian and Siobhan.

of FFC (see Community Service on page 126). Meanwhile South African television offers Fulham's matches in our hotel room, not that the results bring any comfort. P3 L3, thus points gained nil, and we are still in the relegation

Back to school – Harrodian Colts XV training with Mr Seaton. Our playing fields were used by FFC for many years. (Have a look at page 247 of Johnny Haynes – The Maestro.*)*

zone. Never mind, says Fulham Jim from Tokai. He has been listening to Roy Hodgson on the Cape Town clubline. He assures me that it is going to get better. His Gooner of a father-in-law points to the floor: "Down with the Derby, you're going down with the Derby." Probably so but the dry heat helps ease the pain. Less coughing now and much improved appetite. Time to go home.

Back to school and back to work. Back to Fulham and back to basics; relegation avoidance can begin now that Bullard and McBride are fit again. Back to the Cottage for the Villa match. Worst possible start when the bike broke down at Barnes Bridge, thus a long walk to catch Hughes' own goal to put the Villa ahead. Then McBride and Bullard turned it all around. We win again and we all feel better. Suddenly the x-rays are lighter and brighter. A smile from the consultant: "It was only pneumonia after all... I'm signing you off."

Signing off at Kingston Hospital, signing on at Fratton Park. Two escapes are better than one. Clap, clap, clap, go the clappers. Oh, happiest of happy hours.

Watney's Red Barrel in the background – jobs for the boys in 1958. Right: at home to Derby County in the Watney Cup of 1970.

WHAT WE WANT IS WATNEY'S

WHAT WE WANT is Watney's work – jobs for the boys in 1958. We want Watney's work and we want Watney's play – Fulham playing at Craven Cottage beneath the Watney's sign. Playing Derby in the Watney Cup of 1970. Fulham lost 5–3 after extra time.

What we don't want is Watney's Red Barrel. It was thirsty work humping those kegs and we accepted Watney's Red Barrel (on the house) in the week but not on Saturdays. When Saturday comes it is off to meet fellow fans of Fuller's

and Fulham in The Red Lion at Barnes, or on sunny Saturdays we might prefer one of those riverside pubs near Hammersmith Bridge: The Dove, The Blue Anchor and The Rutland – triumphs of scenery over substance.

Fifty years on Watney's has gone and Budweiser has taken over the Mortlake Brewery but The Jolly Gardeners has survived. It is a Young's house now with two rooms showing Premiership football on Sky. The big room is full of Chelsea supporters but the senior barman is a

Bespectacled youngster 1986; Hammersmith Ender 1996–2008 (still riding with Young's).

The CAMRA crew (Alan and Karen); and The Bricklayer's Arms, SW15 – firm favourite since August 2002.

Fulham fan. We sit together in the small back room much mocked by the boys in blue who shout through to us: "Walk your dog!" every time Fulham concede a goal.

Come the FA Cup run of '75 we moved from the Hammersmith pubs to The Crabtree where our children could play in the garden. The Crabtree remained a summer haunt well into the 90s. Across the road there was a friendly little pizza parlour which the Guard family decorated for our promotion party in May 1997.

Cometh the Tigana, cometh the campaign for beautiful football. Cometh the Quayles, cometh the campaign for beautiful beer. Pressure from this CAMRA crew prompted a move to Putney Bridge and three Young's houses: The Duke's Head, The Boatman and The Half Moon. One of the few compensations for exile to Loftus Road was an Adnam's pub, The Crown and Sceptre. Back home again in 2002 we fell for Becky at The Bricklayer's Arms. Becky has an excellent selection of Timothy Taylor's ales. We enjoyed a quiet corner table for eight until the big screen TV arrived.

ONE FOR THE ROAD

One for the road, two for the rail and three or four on the Intertoto tour. Any away day following the Fulham must include good food, good fellowship and some real ale or fine wine because the football on the road has gone from bad in 2001 to worse in 2006 and 2007. Sanchez drove us to drink. Bitter the bitter then, but at closing time along came Houdini Hodgson, a Moët of a man, with three away wins in succession. Roy of the Rovers deserves more, much more than Watney's Red Barrel.

GOOD BEER GUIDE

The Turf Moor Two have nominated The Cambridge Blue in Cambridge, The Marble Arch in Manchester and The Wellington in Birmingham.

May 1997, Cambridge 0 Fulham 1. We celebrated promotion at The Cambridge Blue and we return there whenever possible. The Abbey Stadium may never be a Premiership ground but all discerning followers of the Fulham should include it and The Cambridge Blue in their pre-season training.

Friendly fixtures in and around Edinburgh justify visits to The Guildford Arms near Waverley Station. Matches involving Meadowbank Thistle, Livingston, and Heart of Midlothian have included goals from Zat Knight and Andy Cole plus a rich range of real ales. My particular favourite is Wildcat from the Cairngorn Brewery.

The Quayles have taken us to some interesting pubs before crunch games in the Premiership. Near the Walker Stadium we enjoyed The Hay Wagon ahead of Leicester 0 Fulham 2 (two spectacular goals from Collins John). Just outside Reading there is a small,

Next stop – Edinburgh Waverley and The Guildford Arms.

quiet pub, The Hopleaf (Hopback Brewery). We were there for late season crisis games in 2007 and 2008. Not so near the ground at Southampton is The Waterloo. We almost missed the kick-off in February 2004 (a no-score bore draw). We might as well have remained at The Waterloo enjoying a pint or two of Summer Lightning – neither thunder nor lightning on the pitch at St Mary's.

Over the hills and far away there was The Blue Moon in Bologna and Zlatco's on the waterfront at Split. At Boban's in Zagreb there were the

sensational red wines of Dingac with which to celebrate Dinamo 0 Ulham 3. Best in Berlin was The Adlon with the poshest loos ever visited on tour with Fulham. (Worst in Premiership: Portsmouth; worst in league: Colchester and Barnet where Wellington boots are advised.)

The Adlon Hotel, Berlin – five-star facilities.

On the left, the best beer for all athletes; on the right, the 'ooh, aah, Tigana' – a very fine wine from a very fine manager.

Following the Fulham into Europe we tended to travel via Ashford or Stanstead rather than Torquay. We have come a long way since Feb 1996 (Torquay 2 Fulham 1). In those days it was "Branfoot out" at The Elephant on Beacon Terrace. KK took us to the play-offs at Cleethorpes (Grimsby red not available) and JT took us back there as champions (Grimsby red still not available). Then we were into Europe via Haka, Egaleo, Sochaux, Bologna, Split, Zagreb and Berlin. Extensive, expensive and well worth every euro; see Alex the Traveller's *A Fulhamish Coming of Age*. Raise a glass of fine white wine to JT (Cassis 1999).

We just missed out on UEFA's Fair Play place in 2008 but there was the Okroju of Korea in July then the Bull Ring for a drink at The Wellington ahead of the friendly/not so friendly with Birmingham.

Off to Jerusalem? Ye Olde Trip to Jerusalem. Founded in 1189 and the oldest pub in the *Good Beer Guide*. Ideal meeting place before fixtures with County or Forest. "You're not famous any more," but Forest are on the way up. We met them in the Carling Cup in November 2004 and we may well see them back in the Premiership very soon. Oh for another trip to Jerusalem.

HEARTS AND MINDS

SOME FULHAM PLAYERS have been natural crowd pleasers who obviously enjoyed the game and wanted to entertain their supporters. The first volume of *Following the Fulham* covered 1951–2001 and the entertainers from those years are easily identified – Tosh, Rodney Marsh, Fred Callaghan, Les Strong, Johnny Mitchell, George Best, Ivor, Big Jim Stannard, Simon Morgan, Hayles, Cookie Coleman, Boa and Saha.

The Premiership years 2001–2008 feature some of JT's crowd pleasers, but Sir Alex snatched Saha, and Boa lost his smile when appointed captain. Inamoto in the Intertoto and Sava in his mask pleased the crowd but not the manager. Jimmy Bullard was an immediate success, playing with a smile, appearing to enjoy each and every game – energetic, enthusiastic, effective and easily the most impressive of CC's signings. A terrible injury kept him out of the game for months but he remained in touch with the supporters and proved as fine an ambassador for Fulham as he had for Wigan.

Other Fulham players engaged the mind more than the heart. They were respected as thoughtful, skilful, influential, valued and valuable. Robson and Haynes, Mullery and Moore, Peyton and O'Driscoll, Gale and Roger Brown, Goma and John Collins are candidates from the years 1951–2001.

The Premiership years demanded intelligence as well as talent, application as well as flair. Finnan and VDS had these qualities but were soon recruited by bigger clubs. Lee Clark was a fine captain until age and injuries limited his appearances. Brian McBride soldiered on and was highly regarded by fans and managers. Again a bad injury had dire consequences for the player and the squad during the 2007–08 season.

Of all the Sanchez signings only Konchesky and Hughes could be seen as successful. Hardly crowd pleasers but competent, diligent and industrious. At the eleventh hour Hodgson recruited a strong central defender – Hangeland – and he certainly made a difference in May 2008. If Murphy is injured or off form, why not pass the captain's armband to Hangeland? Pass the ball to Jimmy Bullard who can get on with playing as he pleases and pleasing as he plays.

In 2008 once McBride and Bullard were fit we could fight our way to safety. With Hangeland and Bullard fit we might even rebuild Fortress Fulham. They demonstrated just what can be achieved in the win over the Arsenal when Fulham, as *The Times* and *The Daily Telegraph* observed, "out-thought and out-fought" the Gunners. The "out-classed and out-passed" tributes are

Crowd pleasers one and all. Clockwise from top left: Jim Stannard, Alan Mullery, Bobby Moore, Louis Saha, Gerry Peyton and Roger Brown.

unlikely to be repeated but we can look to Roy and Ray to out-think most teams with the 'out fighting' to be done by Murphy, Gera, Hangeland and Hughes. Thinking may not be a Bullard forte; free spiriting is our Jimmy – and named now in the England squad. Sing "Jimmy Bullard, international, international, international!"

FROM OUR OWN CORRESPONDENT

JONATHAN SIM – also known as 'The Undertaker' from Fulham's days in the fourth division – has moved from radio to television. He is no longer our

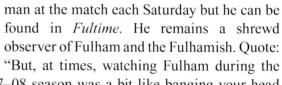

man at the match each Saturday but he can be found in *Fultime*. He remains a shrewd observer of Fulham and the Fulhamish. Quote: "But, at times, watching Fulham during the 2007–08 season was a bit like banging your head repeatedly against a pebble-dashed wall. When it [salvation] finally came in the shape of that glorious Danny Murphy header, my immediate reaction was that it was offside, and there was a strange hiatus as the truth sank in, followed by an inevitable return to my previous taut emotional state: 'Easy, Fulham, easy, just keep hold of the ball… Please…' "

There are some other journalists with a fondness for Fulham. The most distinguished is Brian Glanville, whilst Harry Harris and Danny Fullbrook were responsible for the most detailed account of that first season in the Premiership. David Miller of the Telegraph is strong on atmosphere and ambience.

"To go to Craven Cottage was to laugh a lot." Yesterday's men Michael Parkinson and Denis Compton enjoyed laughing with us but the pundits of today prefer to laugh at us. Lawro has spent 2001–2008 predicting relegation for FFC. When questioned about Liverpool's visit to Loftus Road in 2002 he asserted that Fulham "never ever" beat Liverpool. Match result? Fulham 3 Liverpool 2. Or consider, Mr Lawro, Fulham 2 Liverpool 0 in October 2005, and Fulham 1 Liverpool 0 in April 2007.

Garth Crooks (so often the personal guest of David Roodyn at Craven Cottage) is much given to little jokes about our many mishaps. Sheila pointed this out at one of David's parties. "All good fun, all good fun!" quoth the pundit. Bit of a wag or bit of a drag? Disgusted of Mortlake would prefer some redirection of these jests to thicker skinned fans at Anfield or the Emirates or Old Trafford or Stamford Bridge.

Even less acceptable less was an article *On the Terraces* which appeared in the National Express newsletter. It is both unsavoury and inaccurate. "Not that Al Fayed notices. Bullet-proof glass shields an empty executive box." Thanks to Bill and Andy Muddyman, I have spent many hours in some far from empty executive boxes at Craven Cottage and Loftus Road. Chairman Mo certainly notices; Chairman Mo is not shielded by bullet-proof glass; Chairman Mo is more walkabout than Popemobile.

Most journalists fail to note the twinkle in the eye of our chairman. His remarks about FFC as "the Man Utd of the south" have returned to haunt him. Many pundits longed for our relegation in 2008 although some of the more experienced commentators respected Roy Hodgson's manner and methods. Only Lee Dixon saw any light at the end of the Cottage tunnel.

The BBC invited all three wise men to conduct our last rites on 11th May 2008. They were astonished at the result but warmed to the magnanimity and considered courtesy of Fulham's manager before, during and after the match. No vainglorious "We was well up for it," "We was just too good to go down," or "I told you so."

More obliging than JT, calmer than CC, shrewder than Sanchez, Mr Hodgson might just win over Fleet Street and Broadcasting House. Rudyard Kipling wrote poems about such managers.

Freddie Fulham says: "Pick of the pundits – Tony Gale."

Host with the most? Used to be Jimmy Hill but nowadays it's that Hooray Hartlepool – Jeff Stelling.

"Tony Gale must score..." – and he did against Crystal Palace. Talented young defender then, mature commentator now.

WHERE WERE YOU...

...when we won the championship?
Out of my seat and up in the air.

...when we entered the Premiership?
At my son's wedding, or I would
have been but for Sky moving the
Man Utd fixture to the Sunday.

...when we won our very first Premiership points?
Block T, Riverside.

...when we left the Cottage?
Off to Athens with Derek (below).

...when we went to Loftus Road?
With Ken the editor (right).

...when we entered Europe?
Athens, Sochaux, Bologna, Split, Zagreb, Berlin.

Athens

Split

...when we won the Intertoto Cup?
With Bill Muddyman.

...when we returned home?
In J block with Sheila (and Quigs and Colonel Shrimpton). We were watching FFC v Watford. Ray Lewington (how appropriate) was at the new Craven Cottage for a friendly fixture. Sunny day, warm work, many substitutions (too many substitutions?). Referee abandoned match. No matter – we were home, sweet home.

...when we mourned for the Maestro?
Block T, Riverside. Final score: Fulham 2 Liverpool 0.

...when we seemed to have lost Jimmy Bullard?
In Mortlake listening to the wireless. Alarm calls to Derek and Steven who were there. Final score: Newcastle 1 Fulham 3.

...when we almost lost Brian McBride?
Up and cheering his goal, anxious as he fell so awkwardly, aghast as he was taken away to hospital. Final score: Fulham 1 Middlesbrough 2. (2–2 if you count late equaliser. More misfortune for Sanchez. Healy's 'goal' shown again and again on *Match of the Day*.)

...when we waved goodbye to Sanchez?
In bed. Sick of Sanchez and feverish with flu. I was asleep at the time. The phone rang and Sheila took the call from Brian Gee, a pupil of mine in '75 and a long suffering follower of the Fulham. He flew to Newcastle for the Carlisle game and sat with me at Loftus Road once, just the once, as his knees couldn't take the strain. Brian's message: "Sanchez sacked." Succinct. Brian then rang Haverhill with an extended, well documented analysis of Fulham's past, present and future.

Lawrie Sanchez: Should he stay with Northern Ireland, should he go to Fulham? (Dunno, but he should've gone to Specsavers...!)

I had taken my leave of Mr Sanchez after the Wigan game on

22nd December. He made me ill, very ill, indeed so ill that I had to go to Africa to find the dry heat which cures such agues.

...when we warmed to Roy?
At Newlands cricket ground, over the hills and far away. Press reports and interviews suggested that this man had class. I was convalescing outside Cape Town with Tokai Jim and we listened to Clubline. We both took to the manner and the message. Articulate.

Listening to reasoned exegesis helps but seeing is believing. Ecce, behold the return of the passing game, it is the end of hoof-it. After 22 games in the relegation zone FFC are climbing learning's ladder, after 134 away games FFC achieved not one, not two, but three away wins. Houdini Hodgson.

...when we saved the day?
At Fratton Park behind the goal. On the beach, grinning from ear to ear (still grinning actually).

When we saw the fixtures for 2008–09?
On the pitch. On the Harrodian pitch where Johnny Haynes listened to Bobby Robson, and Ivor laughed with Les Strong (and I worked with Simon Morgan).

Fixture list kindly delivered to the pitch by golf trolley; thanks, Dave, and thanks, John. "Let's get ready for Hull."

SIMPLY THE BEST

SIMPLY THE BEST, as sung by Tina Turner, heard around the grounds but seldom seen on the pitch. In my 57 years following the Fulham, all too often it has been just that. More Heinz than Harrods – 57 varieties – and only under Tigana, P10 W10, did we see sustained quality of performance. That was our season of seasons, the 2000–01 team was indeed simply the best but it was not a Premiership team. Our performances 2001–2008 have been Heinzish and Fulhamish but there have been some golden games.

I offer in evidence six of the best.

SIX OF THE BEST – Home games

Bolton, August 2004
Fulham 2 Bolton 0 – Back home.

Norwich, May 2005
Fulham 6 Norwich 0

Liverpool, October 2005
Fulham 2 Liverpool 0

Chelsea, March 2006
Fulham 1 Chelsea 0 – Worth waiting for, since October 1979.

Arsenal, November 2006
Fulham 2 Arsenal 1 – Worth waiting for, since January 1966.

Birmingham, May 2008
Fulham 2 Birmingham 0 – The noise.

AWAY DAYS – which must be attended in person.
Fulham have recorded some impressive wins at Newcastle and I have watched these matches on TV with Sheila and Piers but they do not count in this survey. Thus although Newcastle 1 Fulham 4 in November 2004 may feature in your collection of great away games it can't be part of my Premiership pilgrimage.

SIX OF THE BEST – Away games

Split, September 2002
Split 0 Fulham 1 (Steed) – For the atmosphere.

Zagreb, October 2002
Dinamo 0 Ulham 3 (Boa, Marlet, Hayles) – For the score and the scoreboard.

Spurs, August 2003 – courtesy of David Roodyn with thanks.
Spurs 0 Fulham 3 (Hayles 2, Boa) – Best of Bazza.

Man Utd, October 2003 – courtesy of David Roodyn with thanks.
Man Utd 1 Fulham 3 (Clark, Steed, Inamoto) – Perfection.

Chelsea, December 2006
Chelsea 2 Fulham 2 (Volz, Bocca) – Almost nicked it, almost October 1979 revisited.

Portsmouth, May 2008 – courtesy of Piers with thanks.
Portsmouth 0 Fulham 1 (Murphy) – Survival in the Premiership.

SIX OF THE BEST – home and away
The matches above are in chronological order and those who were there will have a particular favourite from the Premiership years. Hard to beat Fulham 6 Norwich 0 for fun in the sun, but the Bolton match was 'back home' and thus even more important than victory over Chelsea or Arsenal. The Birmingham game was crucial to survival in the Premiership and (for once) the noise was sustained throughout 90 minutes. "Loud and supersonic" – *The Observer*.

Portsmouth this May was the most valuable but not the most beautiful. For artistry and impact first prize must go to Fulham 2 Arsenal 1 or Man Utd 1 Fulham 3. The best of the best? Over to you.

STOP PRESS:
September 2008 and some latest scores: Fulham 1 Arsenal 0, Fulham 2 Bolton 1. Two good wins, certainly. Top twenty? Possibly. Six of the best? No.

Steed – midfield threat indeed. One of JT's very best buys. Bazza – journeyman striker transformed by JT's coaching team.

Fulham 6 Norwich 0. Clinical – how unlike FFC.

CAN WE PLAY YOU EVERY WEEK?

A CHANT HEARD at the Hammersmith End (and on many another Kop) when the home team are well ahead, as in Fulham 6 Norwich 0 or Fulham 6 WBA 1.

Can we play you every week?

Everton, certainly, if it is every week at home. Seven wins on the trot at Craven Cottage. Everton away each week? No, thanks! Last Fulham victory at Goodison was on the way to Wembley in 1975.

Can we play you every week?

We did play Nottingham Forest 'every week' early in 1975. Five matches between 12th January and 11th February and six fixtures in all with Forest that season. We had five matches with Hull in that same season of 1974–75, and we now meet them again in the Premiership this season.

We would not want to play the Arsenal away every week. Fulham never won at Highbury and have yet to win at the Emirates Stadium. We have won at Stamford Bridge, and we gave them a fright 2–2 in December 2006. Some Fulham fans would like to play Chelsea every week at Craven Cottage. Memories of March 19th 2006 feature rather too often in songs and on T-shirts.

Goldstone days beside the seaside, beside the sea.

There was a greater victory in November 2006 when Fulham beat the Arsenal at Craven Cottage – and continued joy when we beat them in August 2008.

We have a decent record at home to Liverpool in the Premiership beating them once at Loftus Road and twice at the Cottage. The Haynes fixture was the most memorable whilst the Dempsey-engineered win was the most decisive, saving us from relegation and saving the chairman some money. Hooray, but two cheers rather than three, because the victory secured the managership for Sanchez, thus bad buys and worse results until the winter of our discontent was made glorious summer by Roy Hodgson.

Portsmouth away always has appeal because of the sea air and some pleasant sleepovers at Arundel and at Seaview (I of W). On the pitch there have been three especially memorable matches. December 1983 and a victory 4–1, January 1985 from four goals down to 4–4 at the final whistle, and the recent stomach-churning, nail-biting, season-defining, late, late show of Portsmouth 0 Fulham 1.

There are many other grounds which Sheila and I would happily visit every week in or out of season, an ABC of wonderful places: Athens, Brighton, Bologna, Bournemouth, Cambridge, Cheltenham, Cleethorpes, but few of them are in the Premiership, hence (apart from the lottery of the cup) we are unlikely to play them any week, let alone every week. We are reduced to Portsmouth and Hull as coastal resorts and Liverpool as a city of culture.

The good old Division Three (South) was the place to be for jolly easy journeys and easy jolly journeys. Just look at the fixture list for 1931 – a vintage year for those based in block T seats C 17 and 18. Our very first year started in August 1931 away to Coventry. Then we were off to Torquay*, Luton*, Northampton*, Southend*, Clapton, Norwich, Mansfield*, Brentford*, QPR*, Gillingham*, Crystal Palace*, Reading*, Swindon*, Brighton*, Thames, Watford*, Bournemouth*, Bristol Rovers*. Some of these clubs have been in the Premiership. Where are they now? Some of these clubs (*) have been bread and butter fixtures for as long as I have followed the Fulham (1951–2008).

Many of us know the magic of Mansfield; most of us have mixed memories of Torquay; all of us were in exile at QPR. We've had bread and butter Brentford, sunny away days beside the seaside beside the sea at Bournemouth, Brighton and Southend, grim memories of Gillingham in 1997–98 (Fox), a wonderful performance on ice at Swindon, Twerton days playing Bristol Rovers, the pitch collapsing under Big Jim Stannard at Northampton. And an earlier (yes, Steve Earle-ier) great escape at Northampton with Dave Pearce dancing on the pitch in April 1966 and still dancing at Fratton Park on May 11th 2008. We have all danced beside the Thames on our way home from victories at the Cottage, but perhaps only Alex the Traveller watched FFC at Thames FC and Clapton.

By strange good fortune we had friendly fixtures with two of those Division Three South teams this summer: Crystal Palace and Southend. The Dougie Freedman Testimonial match was a must because he so nearly came to Fulham. Fees were agreed but personal terms were supposed to include a second-hand mini for Dougie. We were skint so he went to Selhurst Park. A Marlet moment from our darker days.

Old Fulhamites such as Sharon Duce and Dominic Guard (pictured here) would claim that we were much happier then because it was our club. When Wilkins and Keegan replaced Adams at Fulham, Sharon and Dominic departed with him. Chris Guard has remained on board and we have wondered together at the beauty of the Arsenal. Half-time November 2006 – Fulham 2 Arsenal 1. Chris assured me that the Arsenal would pass us to death in the second half – "They're so ******* good." They didn't that night, but they usually do, and they certainly did last season. Chris is a big fan of Jimmy Bullard and informed me that he was off to kiss him after the Villa goal.

The Premiership 2001–2008 has made away days increasingly expensive, hence the temptation to remain at home in front of the television. Not so much 'play you every week' as pay you every week. Pay as you view on Sky or Setanta. 'Twas not ever thus. There was a golden age of travel with Thamesbank, there were outings with Mary the Doughty. But even Jonathan (The Undertaker) Sim only managed one away game last season.

Until late April 2008 following the Fulham around the Premiership grounds was just too painful. Painful to our pockets and painful to our pride. The Reading, Man City, Portsmouth results may moderate the pessimism of the last three seasons. Chairman Mo has subsidised planes, trains and coaches. Top man Topley has attempted to revive the journeymen of '97 and Hull away was sold out within 24 hours, but how many followed the Fulham back to Blackburn in late September or Everton in November?

We went everywhere with Adams and Tigana – perhaps, perhaps Houdini Hodgson will get us out of our armchairs and back on the road.

Back on the road again. COYW.

ABSENT FRIENDS

AN ABC of Fulham friends and Friends of Fulham. Some known, some well known and some unknown.

A is for Alex. Alex the Traveller. Been everywhere with Fulham and told the tale.

B is for Best – a hero of an earlier escape when bottom of the table Fulham beat top of the table Chelsea – plus a patron of Fulham 2000.

B is also for Barbara B. Loyal supporter these may years and champion vendor of tickets for Cottage Chance and Fulham Flutter. Why is such an ever present among the absent friends? Many photo calls but no portrait of Barbara. Ken, Ken, just one would have done, and Barbara would have been on page 72 with the Golden Girls.

C is for Cyril. Cyril Swain was a director during the 1986–87 to 1996–97 rescue operation. Cyril didn't live to see Fulham playing in the Premiership but his widow and daughter remain Riversiders and friends of Fulham.

D is for Davies – Ivor the Engine Davies. Never made the Premiership with FFC but an absent friend in the best sense, always happy to return to the

Cottage. Waves and smiles, smiles and waves.

E is for Emily, once of Fulham, now with Chelsea.

F is for the flags by the river. Golden days with the golden boy (right).

G is for Gary Piper, our chaplain, who has done so much for the bereaved of Fulham when the right

words are needed. FTID – and then instruct executors, relatives and friends to seek Gary's wisdom and loving kindness.

H is for Henry (Brailsford Henry). More Pride Park than Fulham these days but many the phone call to ask after FFC.

I is for Ian – better known as Sammy the Steward. Keeper of the peace at the Hammersmith End

"Now we bring our children."

J is for Jim Lillywhite. Veteran wordsmith and a lovely man.

K is for our Kop. The Kop that was. It has gone but we remain and now we bring our children and grandchildren.

L is for Les. Les Strong, another absent friend. He missed the cup final (through injury) but he captained us to promotion. One of those footballers who used to play with a smile. Still smiling is Les; he often helps David Hamilton on match days and he can be counted upon for the launch of any good cause. Happy days *are* here again, with Les aboard. Recently seen on the Johnny Haynes evening at The Cottage SW6. Still smiling along with Super Mitch (see page 77).

M is for Mary. Little mother of all our away supporters.

I could go on from N to Z. From Norwich Pete who saved us this season by playing golf throughout the last three away fixtures. Walking with him after FFC 2 Birmingham 0, Norwich Pete explained his key part in Roy Hodgson's rescue plan. "I stay away and Fulham stay up." No wonder we lost in Berlin. Norwich Pete was there. Without him we might have won the UEFA Cup.

From N to Z and that night in Zagreb. What no F In Fulham? F you, absent friend. Perhaps you were playing golf with Norwich Pete while Ulham got on with the job. Dinamo Zagreb 'the bad boys in blue' 0 – Ulham 3. The Traveller was there that night. He rests now in J block with Mary the Doughty and Jim the Lillywhite. Please keep a place there for Sammy the Steward.

FOLLOWING THE FULHAM INTO EUROPE

THE SUMMER of 2002 revisited during the summer of 2008. The Intertoto campaign began as a bit of a laugh. Edwin van de Sar had a real medal from the Champions League and insisted on the importance of playing in Europe but Haka was hardly the Juventus he knew and loved.

Participation in the Intertoto tournament brought some unlooked for benefits. QPR were not ready for us in early July so there were two more

matches at Craven Cottage. Wall to wall sunshine and a goal from Saha (above). Definitely the last goal at the old ground.

Come the semi-final (our second cup semi-final of 2002) Loftus Road was open for Fulham fixtures and Sean Davis scored in the 90th minute. We set off for Sochaux in high spirits and were rewarded with two good goals – the first from Legwinski and the second from Hayles. There had been rumours of WBA interest in Barry Hayles but European football soon reconciled him to FFC.

The first leg of the Intertoto final was in Bologna; a major fixture at a major ground, plus the bonus of the goal of the season as early as August – Inamoto's dramatic debut goal. Even more sensational was Inamoto's hat-trick in the second leg on the 27th of August which secured Fulham's first European title and passage into the first round of the UEFA Cup.

Split, Zagreb and Berlin were big fixtures home and away. They produced some wonderful football and memorable journeys. (Dave Pearce's Croatian adventures became a page turner in *Toofif*.) Following the Fulham into Europe was never regretted by the 300 who were there, but the strain was evident in league fixtures. Yes, we had a flying start against Bolton, and topped the Premiership table (albeit briefly), but come December we were struggling at home and losing to Birmingham and Manchester City. Finally there was humiliation at home in the televised game: Fulham 0 Blackburn 4. This defeat cost Tigana his job in April, but one could argue that those 14

Job done – cup won!

Intertoto / UEFA fixtures were just too much for a relatively small squad.

Others claim that it was the purchase of Marlet which undermined Tigana's relationship with the chairman. Marlet may not have given value for money in the Premiership but his four away goals were essential to our survival in Europe.

Whatever the rights and wrongs of *l'affaire Marlet* it would be tragic if Tigana was remembered for one controversial transfer when he gave us the best football ever seen at Craven Cottage and delivered 101 points, promotion to the Premiership, two trophies and European football. Genius.

Marlet's first Premiership goal, December 2001. Fulham 2 Manchester United 3.

ACME THE THUNDERER

IN THE SPRING of 1960 Johnny Haynes completed his 300th first team appearance and Melvin Tenner was well into his third season as a Fulham supporter. I was following from afar as an apprentice schoolmaster at a country boarding school. The head of games there was an old soldier, with many a medal from the Great War. He issued me with my very first Acme Thunderer – it hangs around my neck to this day. I never go to school without it. Indeed I never leave home without it.

Fulham 2000, with Melvin Tenner as mastermind and JH as patron.

Mouthpiece much chewed, in need of a decoke, but still capable of a fierce blast. A blast still to be heard across the 25 acres of the old FFC training ground in Barnes, now my school.

My refereeing days are numbered but I know a good referee when I see one. Remember our UEFA adventure? That thunderer in Zagreb could tell his red cards from his yellow. Then there was the Berlin fixture which warranted the attentions of Maestro Collina – and did the players realise it? Oh yes, they did! No crowding the maestro. Decisions taken, decisions accepted, decisions respected – respect indeed for the referee of referees, simply the best, the acme of thunderers.

Fulham fan Anthony Digby Ellison is a distinguished referee with national and international experience. A Riversider now, he has been known to comment on Mr Halsey's use of the whistle. Not an Acme man that Mr Halsey.

In row D of block T of the Riverside sits Ronnie. With Ronnie on fire it is difficult to understand why CC termed Riversiders "mute". Ronnie sits and

In the 1860s, Joseph Hudson, a trained toolmaker, converted his humble washroom at St Marks Square, Birmingham, which he rented for 1s. 6d a week, into a workshop. Here he did anything he could to supplement the family income from watch repairing to cobbling shoes - and producing whistles. The Acme whistles are the finest whistles manufactured today.

Maestro Collina in charge. FFC v Hertha Berlin, December 2002.

stands, Ronnie leaps and gesticulates. Ronnie is another expert referee, at least I assume he is expert because he obviously sees more than most of us. He is quick to correct the vision of Premiership officials. (Like Mr D'Urso at Ashford, Ronnie can see in the dark.) All the referees have been questioned and apparently most lack parents. Especial attention is reserved for Mr Styles. Commentary on this referee's performance is frequently more entertaining than the match itself. Nor are linesmen exempt – "Nice one, lino! Nice one, son! Nice one, lino! Are you on a bung?"

I have been tempted to offer Ronnie Riverside my Acme Thunderer. With Ronnie in charge we might have retained that penalty which was awarded against the Arsenal. Awarded but retracted at the urgent behest of the Gooners and their on-field arbitration panel. And Healy's unofficial 'goal' against Middlesbrough might have been authenticated.

If Mr Ellison or Mr Ronnie Riverside had been refereeing throughout the Premiership years we would have had many more home wins. Indeed with FFC safe by Easter there would have been little need to travel to Portsmouth; to their credit, of course, Anthony and Ronnie did travel on 11th May 2008. Anthony talked me through it all again at Southend-on-Sea in July – and as for Ronnie Riverside? Ronnie was one row behind me at Fratton Park and in full-throated roar, passionate and partial, drowning out the Pompey chimes.

"Nice one, Ronnie, nice one, son; nice one, Ronnie, let's burst another lung!"

ALL THE GOODIES IN THE COTTAGE PIE

A TRIBUTE, NOT to the magazine produced by the supporters' club, but a tribute from November 1974. The *Sunday Express* match report on Fulham v  Aston Villa. The author was cricket's golden boy and no mean footballer, Denis Compton (left). Denis was to Middlesex and England cricket what Johnny Haynes was to Fulham and England football. Both made the game look easy, both were exquisite craftsmen and both enjoyed massive popularity – legends and Brylcreem boys.

Denis enjoyed his visits to Craven Cottage and was generous in his praise for our veterans Mullery and Moore. That November, however, his man of the match was Les Strong: "It can't be long before this talented youngster gets called into the England squad." It was an entertaining game with Fulham scoring three goals (Lacy, Busby and Lloyd) to Villa's one. An important victory for Fulham because Mullery in his Captain's Column was muttering about the relegation zone. In fact we started a good run of results which blossomed into our FA Cup final appearance at Wembley. Villa bounced back to join Manchester United in gaining promotion. But whilst Villa went forward to European honours, Fulham sat back and smiled after losing the cup final.

Denis Compton was right about those goodies in the Cottage Pie. My son and I enjoyed that match and many others on the way to Wembley. We continued to go together to the Cottage right through the Ivor era. My son then lapsed at university while playing rugby football for Rosslyn Park. Recent excitements at Reading, Man City and Portsmouth have revived his interest in FFC, so we invested in an extra season ticket. We looked forward to the new season and yet more goodies in that Cottage pie.

The Aston Villa fixture in November 1974 was the first match attended by my son Ian. My godson Christopher made his first visit to Craven Cottage in December 1975. Ian and I took Christopher to watch George Best. We stood together in the enclosure for the Millwall and Bolton matches. Christopher was a Villa supporter then and Villa were well on their way to promotion and European honours.

When Fulham joined the Premiership I suggested to Christopher that we might watch the Villa match together but alas Christopher had moved on from Villa to Chelsea. Failed as a father – my daughter Amanda turned her back on Fulham and married into Chelsea. Failed as a godfather – Christopher chose Chelsea.

Recent matches with Aston Villa have been as exciting as November 1974. Goals plenty in December 2005 (3–3). McBride scored twice for Fulham. The goal of the season came in the Villa match of February 2003. We won 2–1

thanks to a howitzer from Harley. A February 2005 fixture included two Angel penalties saved by VDS and a late, late goal from Lee Clark. Last season Villa were on a good run when they came to the Cottage and we were down in the relegation zone. Result: Fulham 2 Villa 1 – a vital victory, McBride and Bullard compensating for the Hughes own goal.

All the goodies in the Cottage pie last season? Certainly and the very best of those goodies at the Hammersmith End.

Right: Villa fan William was guest of PFT in February 2003 and witnessed the Harley howitzer. Goal of the game, goal of the season.

WE ARE SURVIVORS

FROM DAVID ROODYN

Fulham's return to the Premiership unfortunately coincided with my near death. Prior to the first game against Sunderland I saw a surgeon regarding an abscess. We delayed removal for a week as I did not wish to miss the match and in that time I contracted the human flesh disease. Thanks to a superb man called Simon Withey, and 32 operations later, I was at Craven Cottage for the Newcastle game, coincidentally enough on the same date this year. I remember once asking Simon when I was in intensive care with twenty tubes going into me whether I could go to Charlton v Fulham. I can still can see his look of amazement as I was not even off the

critical list! After it was all over I spoke to Jimmy Hill who survived a five-hour cancer operation and his comment said it all: "We are Fulham fans, we are survivors."

I do not think Mr Al Fayed has been given enough credit for keeping the club at Craven Cottage. I run a Fulham luncheon club called The 1879 Club of which Mr Al Fayed is the patron and have thanked him for this. One thing is he is no fool and he must realise that with gates of 25,000 it's going to be tough to get his investment back. A more commercially flint-eyed owner would have moved us out.

THE 1879 CLUB

The Business Club for Fulham Supporters

GUEST OF HONOUR
Chris Coleman

My favourite moment in the Premiership was spent with the author. Bizarrely we were in a tree surgeon's box at Old Trafford and even more bizarrely Fulham won 3–1. Peter, ever tactful, left the VIP box after every goal, and I joined him outside for stifled celebrations. Chris Coleman's Fulham had beaten Manchester United on merit – it does not get much better than that.

FROM THE GREEN POLE, 2001–2008

SCRAWLED ON a wall in Stevenage Road is this text: "FFC. Not so much a programme, more a way of life." A dated tribute in faint and faded lettering but still proclaimed by those supporters who gather by the Green Pole at the Hammersmith End. They have their own fanzone to proclaim their devotion to all things Fulham.

There is a lavishly illustrated account of the 2004 return to Craven Cottage and a selection of songs for Fulham. The sights and sounds so poignantly celebrated by Green Pole TV put the turmoil of these Premiership years into perspective.

Consider the Green Pole film: *2004?* 2004? It is not about this or that player, this or that match result, this or that "we was robbed, referee." It is about our life together at home sweet home. Look and learn, watch and weep.

2008? "Going down, going down, down with the Derby." Perhaps – and a pity – but Derby can take pride in Pride Park and we can take pride in the refurbished Cottage. Remember life in the Loft and give thanks for Chairman Mo's 2004–08 Craven Cottage. As John Lennon says/sings on the Green Pole TV: "Our life together – we have grown, we have grown, we have grown!"

Turn over from images of Craven Cottage to Green Pole's song for Fulham. Sit back and listen to golden oldies in honour of Craven Cottage and the fans. More scenes set to music. What scenes! What music! The Traveller and the travellers are 'rocking all over the world'. Intertoto and Inamoto plus the Pope with his FFC scarf.

From the fans on tour scrapbook to those same fans back on the balcony at the Cottage. Next up is Fulham's own singer, songwriter Ralph McTell, serenading the streets of Fulham: "I'll show you something to make you change your mind." Change your mind about going to Stamford Bridge or Loftus Road? Farewell to Finlay Street? NEVER.

Tina Tuner's *Simply the Best*. Simply the best images of the ground by the river, the walks through Bishop's Park, and the views of Hammersmith End "jam packed and on song". Pictures of the team of teams from the season of seasons in 2001 (simply the best ever?). Plus the players in action up at Old

Trafford, Man Utd 1 Fulham 3. Goal scenes with Clark, Steed and Inamoto. Simply the best away performance from the Premiership years?

Perhaps the very clever, very kind people at Green Pole will add the scenes and sounds from May 2008 – Fulham 2 Birmingham 0. Get out your LG clappers, crank up the volume! And the scenes and sounds from Fratton Park on 11th May? Simply the best, better than all the rest.

Tune in to Green Pole TV and you will smile. Is it *Toofif* set to music? Is it *The Sound of Music* from a Riverside Studio? The sound of FFC music and the sound of COYW music illustrated with scenes of the Fulham family, for the Fulham, by the Fulham family. All the goodies in the Cottage pie set to music. Sing along, sing along!

Sing along with JT and CC, sing along with Roy and with Ray. But sing a song of Sanchez? In *Toofif* perhaps, but *not* on Green Pole TV.

Status Quo on the status quo An end of season report for May 2008. As things stand at 5pm on 11th May the Status Quo verdict is: "I like it, I like it. I like it, I like it… I li-li-like it, I li-li-like it!"

BACK HOME – AUGUST 2004

"I AM SURE that you are as pleased as I am to be back here and it is my aim to make this a stadium of which we can all be proud." – *Mohamed Al Fayed.*

Ian McCulloch reported: "I was lucky enough to get a sneak preview of the newly refurbished Craven Cottage a couple of months ago. There was a lot of feverish building work going on, but the old place was unquestionably and

breathtakingly a new ground. To discover it miraculously dragged into the twenty-first century, but still utterly and undeniably The Cottage, almost brought a tear to my eye. This is still Craven Cottage, a ground of immense character and charm, a stadium with a cottage in one corner and a bloody great tree in the other, and a stadium where the river laps down one side."

Nick Wood, season ticket holder, enclosure, 1975 to 2008: "Craven Cottage is as much a part of the experience on a Saturday as any player or team put out by the club. It's unique in the Premiership. Results were good

"That bloody great tree."

at Loftus Road, but the Cottage has that special atmosphere which can exert a powerful hold. It's great that the ground is full again and that the whole place has been brought back to life."

And from the *Doneraile Milkman*, a giant of a goalkeeper who was called up by Fulham when Jim Stannard went missing (taller than Jim, faster than Jim and still going strong in the enclosure): "I love the idiosyncrasies of the Cottage. For example, in the Stevenage Road stand take a right immediately after you are through one of the turnstiles and go through the unmarked wooden door and there is a gents that is always empty. You wouldn't get that at a new build ground."

STORM IN A D CUP

SOMEWHERE BETWEEN Loftus Road and Craven Cottage we lost the voice of Fulham. David Hamilton had been our DJ and MC for years and years. It was all aboard his plane to Manchester for the semi-final replay in 1975. It had been all the way to Wembley with David, and all the way up and down the divisions with David. He had talked us through hundreds of games with a style and a smile unmatched at any other football club. A class act, far and away the best MC in all the divisions. A Premiership performer even when we were 91st and looking into the Conference. David helped us survive the Dark Ages and he hosted our celebrations under KK in 1999 and JT in 2001. David was looking forward to leading us out of exile in August 2004. David was the man with the right words for our return to Craven Cottage. Public orator and voice of Fulham – your hour has come!

We duly assembled for the friendly with Ray Lewington's Watford. The ground looked good, the ground looked grand but what was that awful sound and who was that mumbling at the mike? Not David Hamilton and not good enough. With each friendly game came another trialist MC. Each one inarticulate and inaudible. There were protests, of course, and Disgusted of Tunbridge Wells wrote in, phoned in, moaned in, but all in vain. Local and national newspapers carried the story. I remember a pre-match lunch at the SW6 branch of ASK. David had to leave the table for photographs and interviews. Farewell to Finlay Street! Hello to Fleet Street!

Come the official opening of Craven Cottage and the first home game in the Premiership (the home again game for the Fulham faithful) David was there but *not* as MC. Instead it was the special one, the chosen one, the frisbee of frisbees, Dominic (the debutant) Frisby. Mr Dominic Frisby claimed to have supported Fulham for years as he warmed us all up for the chairman's walkabout and our opening hymn *Back Home* by Clive Allen with Chairman Mo as lead singer.

The sun was shining and we all joined in. *Back Home!* Back home indeed and time for CC's team to show their appreciation of the new pitch and the

refurbished Cottage. Bolton were seen off 2–0 – a double from Andy Cole. How appropriate as he had known the crumbling old ground in lower division days and could appreciate the transformation – a Premiership Cottage for a Premiership Fulham.

Everyone happy? Smiles all round? Well, not quite. Very few smiles in the directors' box. Chairman Mo was not amused. Chairman was about to chuck the Frisbee. Goodbye, Dominic. Come back, David Hamilton. Welcome back, Diddy Dave! Business as usual 2004–2008.

Good old Mr Articulate – the Voice of Fulham – *multum in parvo* – our very own mini maestro – David Hamilton, back home. Back home where he belongs *and* here to stay.

Job for life, says Chairman Mo – and so say all of us.

LOOKING GOOD

A HOMILY ON away days with the Fulham – "when bookworms take wings and footnotes can fly."

Historians are all too often library bound. Hours and hours among the archives; once it was dusty documents, now it is microfilm. The Wren Library at Cambridge is gracious and spacious, more gracious and spacious than Colindale but both force the head down. Head down most of the time, spirits down some of the time. In the slough of despond? World weary? Word weary?

Take a break, have an away day linked to your research topic, get out and about; shake a leg, open your eyes. Look up not down, look and learn.

In 1966, when George Cohen was preparing for Wembley, I took a group of sixth-formers to the Tudor galleries at the V and A. The guide, Elizabeth Makepeace, greeted us with these words: "Forget those text books; I am here to open your eyes. Stand and stare. Do not look down reading labels; look up and behold the beauty of these Tudor treasures. Learn to look and soon you

A Cambridge library and an Oxford college – all part of following the Fulham around the lower league grounds.

will be singing *Sursum Corda*. The sooner you learn to lift up your eyes, the sooner you will lift up your hearts."

How right she was in 1966, and acting on her advice we went walkabout and look about to Ingatestone Hall, a Tudor masterpiece on the road to Southend-on-Sea. Many a time has a match at Edgar Street included dalliance with Hereford's mappa mundi; or there was the oblique approach to the Abbey Stadium via the chapel of King's College; and at Oxford the old Manor Ground was all the better for a morning in Tom Quad or beneath the Radcliffe Camera.

Premiership grounds are seldom within walking distance of universities or cathedral cloisters. Hence the general delight when Southend-on-Sea challenged FFC to a pre-season friendly fixture. A chance to revisit Ingatestone Hall before taking a stroll along the sea front; blow away that document dust, take wings, oh ye bookworms! Fly, fly, ye footnotes! Look and learn from the Shrimpers.

Programme Pete exhausted from the Colindale archives; Anthony escaping from A level scripts; PFT a wary and weary proofreader. All three more than ready to take the cure at Southend-on-Sea.

Hot from the press – the Ashwater Press – some proof pages of this collection of essays on Fulham's Premiership years. So far, so promising, and a fair read, or so it seemed, on the train to Southend. Proofreading done, it was off to the sea front to admire the famous pier.

Inevitably (and delightfully) I bumped into several followers of the Fulham from seasons past. Among them Dave Pearce, fresh as a daisy from Portsmouth in May 2008 and Northampton in 1966. Immediately I tracked back to Ken Coton's *Golden Years* page 63 and a photo which captured the relief and

Dave Pearce dancing on the Northampton pitch in 1966. Dave Pearce (30 years on) watching 92nd-placed Torquay beat 91st-placed Fulham and looking into the Conference.

amazement of that particular escape. Forward to page 96 of *Following The Fulham*. Look at the tension and despair on the faces there.

Two away day tales which may read well but where the point is sharpened, honed, polished and underlined by the right image – the photo to compliment and complement.

Fulham's wordsmith (be he Turner, White, Plumb or PFT) is half the man without the Coton camera. Dave Pearce prefaced a discussion of the Haynes book with the comment "magnificent photos". This point was well made at Southend (beside the seaside beside the sea). Good as the football might or might not have been on the evening of 14th July 2008, the occasion would have been heightened by "capturing the passing scene," Ken's very own phrase for a concept enshrined in a volume of such scenes: *Fulham Photos.*

The same point was put another way that same evening at Southend: "Just look at that pier," and later after leaving the seafront for Rootes Hall: "Just look at that sunset." In the Golden Eagle I shared a glass with Programme Pete who had spent the morning in the Colindale archives researching half-time scores from 1939. He is helping Dennis Turner with some footnotes. We all learn from footnotes but detail benefits from apposite visual aids.

Once inside the Rootes Hall car park (massive) I chanced upon Anthony Ellison a close companion from the Riverside block T (Anthony is a much travelled athlete, referee and senior examiner). "Just look at that sunset!" quoth the expert chemist, fresh from a thousand marking schemes. Up went my camera (where is Ken when you need him?). Concise and cogent analysis of Cook's contribution to this entertaining friendly fixture is of interest to supporters who waited many months for a contribution from the legend of Loftus Road but the comments of both Anthony and Dave prove that mere words are not enough.

Southend-on-Sea

Reading is necessary, proofreading very necessary, but seeing is believing. Hence "Look at that sky" (be it sunrise in Bishop's Park or sunset at Southend-on-Sea). Again and again over the years I have called out to followers of the Fulham: "Just look at Ken's photos from Hull in September 1975." The first defines the moment, the latter fixes the place.

Enough of proofreading, now for the real joy of chronicling the Premiership years – the placing of the images. The images which turn looking promising into looking good. Often thanks to Ken or Alan Williams or Sheila, the photos save the page. Now and again the right photo, the exact image, turns looking good into looking great. Conversations with Dave Pearce, Programme Pete and Anthony Ellison are an important part of chronicling the Premiership years but happy snaps preserve the moment for those who were there. The right visual aid can transport those who were not present. A comfort zone with consolation prizes for those who missed the magic of Mansfield in April 1997 or the glory of Old Trafford in October 2003 or the tension at Fratton Park in May 2008, or even the promise, the buzz, of another new season.

A warm glow on a warm evening as we launched the new season at Southend-on-Sea, July 14th 2008.

This is what we used to enjoy in our match programmes. Left: a goalscorer, a ball entering the net – a golden goal from a golden cameraman. (Barry Lloyd at Hull in September 1975.) Right: a scene from the match which captures the ambience, as John Mitchell puts his best foot forward at the railway end of Boothferry Park. Such images are seldom seen in Premiership programmes. Mourn as we must the loss of Ken's camera, we are not left comfortless. Ormondroyd is assembling a brilliant collage of life in the Premiership.

Jake Murray, a photographer and Nottm Forest supporter, has helped me with a number of projects in and out of school. That's him pictured above at Harrodian. By way of thanks I gave him a copy of *Following the Fulham Around the Grounds*. His comments were telling. Not a word about the Thomson text but many tributes to Coton's photographs. "Look at the crowd on the terraces at Hillsborough" (page 98). Jake copied and enlarged Sandra's photograph of Mary Doughty at Cambridge in May 1997. Ken saw the resulting image (below) and immediately suggested it for the cover of this book – Mary looking good on that carnival of a day for followers of the Fulham. Perhaps not right as the cover of a volume on the Premiership years but perfect for an essay on Fulham's golden girls. Mary looking good, Mary looking great.

WORSE THAN THE YEOVIL

IN THE *Sunday Telegraph* of 28th August 2005, David Miller wrote:

Fulham 1 Everton 0. I have seen Yeovil perform better than the winners. For Fulham, relegation avoidance begins in August. Yes. It is that bad.

A shame that the match should be so mundane, Adjacent Bishop's Park shone in the sunshine beside a sparkling Thames. Craven Cottage was brimming with its traditional goodwill. There is an endearing kind of provinciality about Fulham, free of all expectation, indulging with gusto in chants ten years out of date. Grateful for anything even approaching entertainment.

Quite so. For many of us provincials Craven Cottage is more than the Premiership. Naturally our chants are ten years out of date. We are still living the great escape from the Conference with our favourite manager Micky Adams and our favourite captain Simon Morgan.

2001 was merely dreamtime with JT and Saha – never before such football from Fulham and probably never again. It was possible in the first division but it didn't work in the Premiership. To be honest *we* don't work in the Premiership. It is all too earnest, solemn, serious and stressful. True it was good beating Man Utd at Old Trafford – a mighty performance – but we all knew it didn't really mean much. We were never going to sustain such results.

For many of us Carlisle, Mansfield and Cambridge in '97 were the great away days. Read *On Song For Promotion* by Simon Morgan for authentic FFC – provincial and proud of it. Every ground was different then and every away match was a real day out (often the outing was better than the football). Give me Bournemouth over Birmingham, Blackpool over Blackburn, Brighton and Hove Albion over West Bromwich Albion. Of the Premiership grounds only Portsmouth offers old fashioned adventure. Fratton Park may be a dump but it is a genuine bricks and mortar dump with plenty to do before and after the match – historic ships or the Isle of Wight ferry. As for the rest of the Premiership, having done the rounds of those giant plastic superdromes it is easier on the soul (and on the pocket) to slump in front of the TV. The Sky is the limit.

Back to those dated songs – not so much ten years as 30 years out of date with *Viva El Fulham* taking us back to Wembley in '75. We prefer mellifluous melody to cutting edge cacophony. *Back Home* is another favourite with a catchy tune from all those TV commercials. It is associated with ambrosial rice puddings. Puddings – sweet and creamy puddings. Such comfortable music and words. That's just what we need at Fulham. Comfort food to get us through another season of relegation avoidance. Stoke have *Delilah* and they may need her as they endure the slings and arrows of outrageous fortune/misfortune that is the Premiership.

1958–83. Years in which we concentrated each August on relegation avoidance but somehow reached Wembley by the most protracted route on record. We lost of course and throughout those golden years we won… nothing. Nothing except the loyalty of Johnny Haynes plus the affection of many discerning neutrals. Neutrals who noted the sparkling location, the traditional goodwill and the endearing provinciality of Craven Cottage.

Our chairman for most of those golden years was a comedian, Tommy Trinder. He was not the only comedian at Fulham. There were several on the pitch, such as Tosh Chamberlain and Bobby Keetch. Other wags and wits populated the Stevenage Road enclosure with ample advice for the team in general and Jimmy Hill in particular.

In the summer of 2002 Fulham qualified for Europe. We astonished ourselves and the pundits by winning the Intertoto Cup and advancing on Berlin via Split and Zagreb. Our theme song throughout the seven away fixtures was "Conway, Jimmy Conway, Jimmy Conway on the wing." A song from a previous sortie into Europe – not so much ten years out of date as 28 years past its prime. Jimmy Conway had scored our last European goal in Bologna in May 1974. We were unbeaten in Europe then, and from July to December 2002 we sustained that improbable record.

Relegation avoidance begins in August. Yes – season in, season out for Fulham. Jimmy Conway was part of the Houdini sides from the 60s but Fulham were relegated in 1968 and again in 1969. Conway started with Haynes and survived to accompany Mullery and Moore to Wembley in 1975. Fulham fans loved Jimmy Conway and Jimmy Conway was fond enough of Fulham to send them his talented son Paul in 1994. While Branfoot dithered Knighton pounced; thus when Carlisle came to Craven Cottage that October it was Paul Conway who scored the third and decisive goal. Fulham 1 Carlisle 3. Fulhamish. Wasting opportunities, inconsistent, flattering to deceive, vulnerable and much inclined to self-inflicted wounds. Once upon a time FULHAMISH was our official address for telegrams but today it is our permanent state of mind.

Fortress Fulham? Some fortress! Ask non league-Hayes who dumped us out of the Cup at Craven Cottage in 1991 or Leyton Orient, easy winners in 2006. You suggest that Yeovil are better than Fulham; they certainly were in

1993. Those were the days, beaten home and away by Scarborough. Defeated by Doncaster and struggling for a draw against nine-man Hereford. And it got worse in 1996. Beaten 3–1 by Scunthorpe in front of 2,176 supporters. The lowest league attendance at Craven Cottage and the lowest league position – 91st. Fortress Fulham, indeed!

Brimming with traditional goodwill – and why not? We have so much to be thankful for. We survived (just) and we retained Craven Cottage. For survival we give thanks to Adams and Morgan on the pitch and the Muddymans off the pitch. For Craven Cottage retained and refurbished we give thanks to Chairman Mo.

Bishop's Park shone in the sunshine beside a sparkling Thames. True, very true. Which other Premiership ground enjoys a comparable location? Which other London ground has such glorious surroundings? Which English league stadium can match the setting and the scenery?

Grateful for anything even approaching entertainment. Grateful for survival after the wilderness years – only Rochdale had gone as long without promotion. Grateful for survival at Craven Cottage despite the machinations of first the Clays and then Marler Estates. Grateful for anything even approaching entertainment after years of turmoil and torture. We may never match Yeovil on the pitch but we can share their appreciation of Alec Stock. Back in 1975 we sang for him with gusto "Viva El Fulham". We still sing for

him. We still sing for Conway, for Cohen and for Cookie. We still sing for Ivor, for Morgs and for Mo. With traditional gusto, then, just one more time: "Next year we're going to win the cup (ho, ho), viva el Fulham."

Alec Stock took us all the way to Wembley.

SPONSORS PAST AND SPONSORS PRESENT

LONG AGO OUR main sponsor (year in, year out) would be Deans Blinds. The Deans were directors, their firm picked up the bills. Later on during the crisis of 1986–97 we were rescued by Paul Kenny and the GMB.

The link with GMB was maintained in the Premiership by Tom Greatrex who took such a major part in the BTTC campaign. Premiership Fulham and a rapid turnover: Pizza Hut, Betfair, dabs.com, Pipex, LG. Goodness knows what LG must have thought of their team's away form. Hardly commercial travellers those teams of 2006 and 2007. Indeed LG must have been deeply disappointed both home and away last season. "Down with Derby, you're going down with the Derby."

One LG advertisement was especially appropriate to such troubled times. "The jersey for Christmas – your club is for life." *Your club is for life.* True for many of us. Fulham "to have and to hold, for better for worse, for richer for poorer, in sickness and in health, till death us do part." Between 1951 and 2001 there have been all too many such worse years, poorer years, sickness years and (until Chairman Mo took over) there were more relegations than promotions. The Old Fulham fans have been hanging on in there. "Chin up, grin and bear it – your club is for life." A life sentence? It often seemed so at times for the fans but why should any sponsor stick with it? Paul Kenny must have had difficulty convincing

Paul Kenny of GMB – generous sponsor throughout the darkest days of FFC.

some of his union that FFC equalled anything other than a lame duck or lost cause. When the good times came to Fulham, GMB moved on to help another lame duck at Griffin Park.

LG must have begun to regret that message for Christmas 2007 – *The jersey for Christmas, your club is for life*. "In the bleak midwinter frosty wind made moan." Only one win in seventeen matches to the end of 2007. Relegation form in the relegation zone. Time for a new manager, time for a new message.

The LG marketing men came up with a secret weapon for the crunch game, that 'six pointer' with Birmingham where we used those LG clappers to go from loud to supersonic. "Weapons of mass destruction," according to Karen Brady (Mrs Pesch), who swiftly devised a blue version for her Birmingham's final fixture.

And so to Fratton Park on Super Sunday, 11th May 2008. High noon indeed as many LG clappers travelled down to Portsmouth. A day of intense heat and great tension with many LG clappers serving as sunshades before the match. Fans for our fans turned into instruments of torture for our hosts. The usual Pompey chimes from them, the unusual LG clappers from us.

'Twas a close contest on the pitch, 'twas a close contest in the stands. Come 5pm Fulham had beaten Portsmouth and the LG clappers had outclapped and outchimed the chimers.

Thanks to GMB in 1995–96–97 and thanks to LG 2006–07–08 – you were much more than mere sponsors of the team. You were both the medium and the message. Switch on those Scarlet TVs; perhaps LG will become "not so much a programme, more a way of life."

They were not LG, they were not PC, but the Cravenettes provided memorable half-time entertainment...

LG THE EMAIL

SO MUCH for LG our sponsor, now for LG the email contact.

LG (Bernard Gallacher) is my guide, philosopher and friend at Wentworth. LG has adopted Fulham as his second team. We are both from Scotland. LG has supported Hibs for years (make mine Meadowbank). LG could have been a professional footballer but opted instead for golf. He retains his footballing skills with particular prowess at corners and free kicks. (LG is the Jimmy Bullard of the Brunei Bullets.)

We served together at the Royal Brunei Polo Club between 1987 and 1997 where LG coached on the golf course in the mornings and helped with the football in the afternoon. Back in England we remained in touch and recently

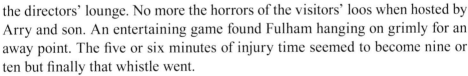

LG has taken two seats in the Riverside Stand. LG and his son Jamie have seen the best and the worst of our Premiership performances. Victories over Liverpool, Chelsea, Spurs and Arsenal have been celebrated, defeats at the hands of Orient in the FA Cup or Sunderland in the Premiership have been endured. Endured but then placed under the microscope by LG.

The morning-after email from LG will make clear where FFC got it right or, more often than not under Sanchez, where FFC got it wrong.

In November 2006 an email from LG contained an invitation to Portsmouth. We enjoyed VIP hospitality in the directors' lounge. No more the horrors of the visitors' loos when hosted by Arry and son. An entertaining game found Fulham hanging on grimly for an away point. The five or six minutes of injury time seemed to become nine or ten but finally that whistle went.

Now the short walk to Arry's Bar. Just time for a quick quote from LG. "Remind me in the next life to choose Celtic and Chelsea. This Hibs and Fulham combination should carry a government health warning!"

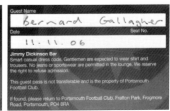

MEANWHILE IN MORTLAKE

MEANWHILE IN MORTLAKE, Fulham's number one window cleaner is walking the towpath with the dogs. The window cleaner meets up with the schoolmaster who is scrounging a seat in front of a Sky set for the next away game.

Alan, Frances and George sailing back to the Cottage, May 2003. Below: three generations of the Mortlake branch of FFC celebrating our first Premiership win – Fulham 2 Sunderland 0 in August 2001.

Eight seasons in the Premiership and many the cup of tea enjoyed chez Gould. Many the cup of tea but few the points gained. There was a 2–2 at Birmingham (thanks to Saha) but never a win when the schoolmaster was in the room. No wonder the dogs bark, no wonder the parrot is sick of his company. He can take a hint, he is off to The Jolly Gardener the next time FFC's away game is on Sky.

The Goulds still talk to the schoolmaster. Together they plan little events of a Fulhamish nature. There was the Magic of Mansfield memorial banquet in April 2007. Together we had endured a miserable afternoon at Reading on the Saturday but were still determined to honour the 10th anniversary of our happier, much happier trip to Mansfield. Ken had prepared the menu's cover page and the Mortlake Hawali served as indicated.

The Mortlake branch of FFC attended: Goulds, Thomsons, Derek and the framers, plus from afar the Bowyer of Brentford, the Woods of Loftus Road and the Lloyds over from Toofif Towers, together with Professor Roodyn who represented the university of Middlesex.

Ken Coton and Derek the Frame at the "Black and White Years" exhibition that supported BTTC. Right: Matthew Lloyd from Toofif Towers, often seen in SW14 where he wears the number 2 shirt as apprentice to Alan Gould, Fulham's number one window cleaner.

Please note that we did not gather in April / May 2008 for some Grimsby Red. We were too busy packing our clappers for Fratton Park.

Meanwhile in Mortlake the parrot has recovered and the dogs do bark. As for Derek and the framers, the window cleaners and the schoolmasters – all still scheming, still dreaming and still in the play-offs, oops, sorry, that was ten years ago – still in the Premiership.

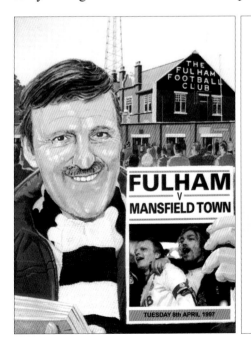

HAWALI MENU

SUNDAY 15th APRIL 2007
7.15pm

Papadum and Chutney

Onion Bhaji
Vegetable Samosa
Chicken or Lamb Tikka Starters

Chicken or Lamb Tikka Massala
Chicken or Lamb Korai
Palak Paneer (V)
Subz Badhami (V)
Bombay Aloo or Mushroom Bhaji or Sag Bahji
Pilau Rice or Plain Nan

Assuming that the YOUNG's house will have answered the
question at 6.30pm
I am providing four bottles house white wine and
four jugs of water for those who do not take to HAWALI
'TIGER'

NB next year at the CAMBRIDGE BLUE...
we must gather for some GRIMSBY RED as we revisit the
joys of the play-offs

THEN AND NOW

Then – agile, accomplished and acknowledged as the Eagle of Eagles (Crystal Palace's leading scorer in the promotion season 1975–76): Dave Swindlehurst, in action scoring a goal against Bolton.

Now – still agile and accomplished, Dave selects the player of the season as senior coach to Harrodian pupils. He remains in touch with Crystal Palace where he has guided youth teams and advised Fulham favourites CC, Kit Symons, Alan Smith and Ray Lewington. Dave assured me in 2000 that Fulham would be promoted by Christmas.

My thanks to Dave for wise words over many seasons and the introduction to Peter Morley. Peter is the Bill Muddyman of Crystal Palace and has the same concern for community service at home and overseas. Peter has provided kit for all the Homestead teams.

Townships, Cape Town

To the boys from the "Homestead Project" keep playing the "Beautiful Game"

Quendenhurst

2004–2005 – Crystal Palace and Fulham together in the Premiership.

2001–2008 – Palace and Fulham together in Cape Town sponsoring Homestead hostels and extending the sports programme for street children.

CRICKET, LOVELY CRICKET

JUNE, JULY AND August used to be for cricket. Many a Fulham player would summer at the Oval. Fender, Ducat and Arnold were England cricketers. As for the rest of the football squad, they had golf to play or gardens to cultivate. As late as 1981 the football kicked off at the end of August. The 29th of the month that year saw us at home to Brentford. Ivor scored with a scorcher of a goal on a scorcher of a day.

Johnny Haynes was with his Winchmore Hill XI in August but would add tennis and golf to the summer cv before returning to football at the Cottage.

That was then. A season was seasonal. Not now. TV talks and it talks football all the year round. July used to be for those lazy, hazy days of summer

July and August are/were for cricket. Johnny Haynes was with his Winchmore Hill XI in July and August.

cricket, but not in the Premiership. In the Premiership Fulham must have high profile fixtures each July. No longer the leisurely GMB tour of Ireland as in 1996. Come 2002 it was European football throughout July. Now it is even more profitable tours of the Far East. China tour last July and Korea tour this July. Home fixtures with Celtic and Rangers have become big business.

Is football in the cricket season here to stay? Yes. More's the pity. At one time last May it looked as if FFC might gain the Fair Play prize. Back in Europe seemed possible but Man City were chosen. Never mind, we needed to concentrate on a steady start, a steady middle and a strong finish.

The glories of the Intertoto and the prestige of UEFA status came with consequences for JT's team. Tired out in December and tumbling down the table. Humiliated at home to Blackburn – beaten 4–0 and all on show as a Sky

fixture, thus public humiliation. Too much football too soon in 2002. Festina lente in 2008? Make haste slowly; pace yourself, Fulham.

Cricket, lovely cricket in late July and early August; those were the days! Steven and Arundel Roger (left) opened the innings at Walton on Thames in 1999, but not in 2002. Steven was in Finland that July following the Fulham into Europe.

PREMIERSHIP CRICKET 1987; PREMIERSHIP FOOTBALL 2007

1987 – 'best of times' with CC

Winning Surrey Cup, June 1987. On tour July 1987 – Brunei and Barbados. Doing the double in Brunei and beating Uppingham in Barbados but losing to Brian Lara's XI.

2007 – 'worst of times' with CC

Following the Fulham around the grounds. An evening with CC – without a win and without a grin.

As tall as Peter Crouch but this CC (below) is Courtney Crouch –

1987 – Winning the Surrey Cup (above); cup double at Jerudong (below).

captain of cricket at Emanuel 1987 and Hammersmith Ender with his mother and brother from an early age. All three anxious throughout 2007 but all three present and correct at Fratton Park in May 2008.

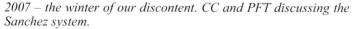

2007 – the winter of our discontent. CC and PFT discussing the Sanchez system.

CC

AS POPULAR AS Ivor, as articulate as Les Strong and as heroic in injury and adversity as Bullard or McBride, Chris Coleman was off to a flying start with the fans when he took over from JT as caretaker manager of Fulham.

On the morning of the Newcastle match, 19th April 2003, Simon Morgan assured me that we would notice a difference. We did. We won and we went on to win again and again – at home to Everton and away to Charlton. Thus Premiership status was preserved and CC was confirmed as much more than caretaker manager.

A flying start indeed and an impressive first full season in charge – 9th in the Premiership and Fulham's best-ever showing at the highest level. One better than May 1960 when Bedford Jezzard took Haynes and Hill, Macedo and Mullery, Leggat and Langley, Cohen and Cook to Old Trafford for a memorable result, 3–3. CC did even better up there, winning 3–1. Thus came to pass Chairman Mo's prophecy "Fulham as the Man Utd of the south." Mission accomplished.

Accomplished for a few hours, but those few hours (plus the top half finish) meant that Chris Coleman was our most successful manager in a hundred plus years.

It couldn't last and it didn't, because CC and Kean were unable to coach the squad into consistency. Defensive errors and howlers away from Craven Cottage meant defeat after defeat from 2005 to 2007. With just two away wins in two seasons the honeymoon was over. Chairman Mo turned to Sanchez.

CC was gone, gone but very definitely not forgotten. The first victory over Chelsea in 27 years, Arsenal defeated for the first time in 40 years and best of all, that afternoon of afternoons at Old Trafford. Thanks, Cookie!

Thank you, Chris, for the public persona and performance, but thanks also for the private concern. Concern for Mary Doughty in her final illness.

Thanks also at a trivial but nevertheless significant level. Manager digs author out of a hole. (A hole of the author's own creation.) Behold one Swansea ticket (opposite). Seeing is believing and I knew that I had purchased this ticket. Purchased certainly, but left on the pin-board in Mortlake. No matter, buy another at the ground. "Sorry, boyo. Sold out." "Sold out! But I have come all the way from London!" "Sorry boyo, still sold out!"

Dash to away team dressing doom and call for Mark Maunders. "Mark Maunders? Sorry, boyo, can't find your McMaunders. Would a local Swansea

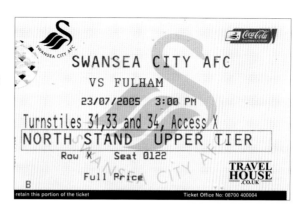

Behold that Swansea ticket – left behind in Mortlake.

boy do instead?" "Do? Do nicely, thank you!" Ticketless Thomson as manager's personal guest. Thanks indeed!

Fool of a pensioner rescued by a generous and gracious player, club captain and manager. Chris Coleman may not have been as good a coach as JT, he may have lacked the experience, wisdom, gravitas of Stock and Hodgson, but he was 'one of us' for eleven years. Our own, our very own boyo, and for three years he delivered more than missing tickets. He delivered "Worth Waiting For" volumes one, two and three. Chelsea, Arsenal and Manchester United on a plate. A plate of gold; yes, solid gold memories. Thanks Chris.

FREDDIE FULHAM

(our No. 1 fan)

says . . .

MY FAVOURITE GRAFFITI

A GREEK WORD from a Greek wall to start us off – "Panathinaikos = Welcome to Hell."

Latin lovers in Bologna responded with "Gianluca Ti Amo." Crabtree fans will recall the wall dedicated to Ernie Howe: "Six foot two, eyes of blue; Ernie Howe is after YOU." (And he scored in the 2–0 win over Chelsea in September 1975.) From that same era: "Chopper Harris, truly horrid. Keeps his bollocks in his forrid." Forehead, methinks. See Freddie Fulham below.

Then there is the scribe of Finlay Street who updates us from year to year and decade to decade: "Mullers is God." No! Ivor is. No! No! Morgs is. No! No! No! Jimmy Bullard is.

Managers are fondly remembered in a Putney underpass: "Dicks out!" "Branfoot out!" "Sanchez out!"

Still singing in SW19 is yesterday's man Rodney. "Who put the ball in the Carlisle net? Rodneeeeeeeeeeee Macareeeeeeeeee!" Ripe for redevelopment as "Who put the ball in the Pompey net? Murphy, Murpheeeeeeeeeeeee!"

From 'Up the Junction' (1983–1994): "Wandsworth women condemn male violence." Answered by: "Battersea boys deplore female graffiti." Local lad from that time Sean Davis must have seen such texts from the railway arch at Clapham Junction.

Freddie Fulham (classicist and heir to the mantle of Merula) says: "Alpha graffiti, omega spelling."

AS OTHERS SEE US

IT IS ALWAYS interesting to read the opposition's programme notes, especially when those comments come from one of our own, one of our own home grown players. Sean Davis is just such a graduate, a Battersea boy who studied at the Micky Adams academy and went on to represent Fulham in all four divisions. In 2001 it was Sean's goals away to Blackburn and home to Sheffield Wednesday that secured our promotion to the Premiership. What would he have to say about Fulham in 2007 and 2008? "I hope this side will again beat the odds and return to Fratton Park for another Premiership tussle." The Pompey pundit's nomination for that Premiership tussle? "FFC's star man is Brian McBride." What about Arry's verdict? "Fulham may not be the most fashionable side, but on their day they are more than capable of causing an upset."

Pompey Pete was less tactful. (An Old Etonian from the 1950s, he is still playing cricket and mixed volleyball.) All elbows and attitude is Pompey Pete. He found me slumped in a dark corner of the Barnes dispensary awaiting treatment. Pompey Pete's treatment? Salt; salt rubbed into wounds. "No hope for you lot! We've got your two best players. Mark my words. Davis and Diop will send you down!"

"Mark my words" indeed and "Mark my words" we did. There was marking, there was learning, there was inwardly digesting and on 11th May we came out fighting. Star man McBride was back, action man Bullard was back – a potent pair for a Premiership tussle. More potent and more polished were they on the day than Pompey Pete's dynamic duo.

Turn to *Freezeframe* photo in *Fultime*. Who is looking in and looking on as Murphy heads home the winning goal? Yesterday's man Sean Davis. As for yesterday's Etonian (Pompey Pete) – "Excuse me, sir, but are you watching on TV?" Are you marking my words?

Are you marking Freddie Fulham's words? "Staying up, staying up, staying up!"

GOLDEN GIRLS

AS IN 2001 so in 2008 it is only right and proper to give pride of place to this photo of Rosemary Shrimpton. The founder's family are still following the Fulham even unto the fourth generation of Shrimptons dancing in Croatia.

Next up a happy snap from Loftus Road just after we had won the Intertoto Cup. Linda with Bill Muddyman. Saviours in 1986–87 celebrating Fulham's triumphal progress through Europe.

A Riversider and a relative newcomer to FFC (above right) but a shrewd judge of character and characters, Mr Parker at work, Bullard and McBride at play.

A seasoned campaigner for Fulham 2000 and BTTC, Sue (below left) organised the first showboat, slow boat, to Greenwich. She was back on board for the Premiership fixture with Charlton in May 2003.

Two golden girls from the Intertoto tour – one (below centre) in Zagreb with her husband (home and away these many years); the other, a more recent recruit, Finnish by birth, Fulhamish by adoption.

Pictured here are more Riversiders celebrating victory over Everton. Formal dress was required for that particular fixture. A bit of a bike ride from the church in Barnes to the Cottage to catch the second half and McBride's winning goal. Back to Barnes for the reception which was held (appropriately) at FFC's old training ground. Sheila calm and composed, the author less elegant but happy for bride (and McBride).

Two more golden girls (below) enjoying promotion in 1997. In May 2008 Sandra celebrated 35 years of distinguished service to the football club and the supporters' club. A blue plaque, a black and white plaque, a golden plaque?

Some proper notice, please, above the entrance to the ticket office.

Meanwhile in Berlin (right), Karen and Elaine prepare for yet another away game following the Fulham. Golden girls at a golden gate. Grander than the gates of Grimsby where I first met Elaine. We suffered in silence in May 1998 as ten man Fulham lost in the play-off up at Cleethorpes. Karen has been secretary to our little group for many a year, organising transport and refreshments for three promotion campaigns, navigating us around the Premiership grounds, looking after us on the Intertoto tour, getting us safely to our seats if we lingered too long over this or that real ale. Thank you, Karen.

And so to Emma, and in a little more detail. Editor of the club programme back in 1994, she had a tiny office and a staff of one. She depended on volunteers for most of the articles. Bob Cain, Jonathan Sim, David Roodyn, Mark Maunders, Magee and PFT all contributed match reports. Emma trained us up and collated our scribblings. We even contrived to win the 1994 'Programme of the Year' award. Jimmy Hill was delighted and invited us to take tea in the chairman's lounge.

Emma was a golden girl then and she is a golden mum now. From Emma Hawkey then to Mrs Tim Miller now. Still devoted to Fulham but no longer locked away in a dark office near Magee's boiler room. I hope Emma has enjoyed these Premiership years. Without her there would have been no programme and thus little documentation of those distant DIY days when we were skint.

Apologies are due to Emma and her mother. We met up after the Barnet match in 1997. I was less than amused with the slope, the loos and the referee. Words were uttered. Words which I now regret. Mr Uriah wasn't listening. The Hawkeys were. Apologies due also to Emma and her husband. I address them as Mr and Mrs Taylor in a previous book. Sorry, Mr and Mrs Miller!

THAT WAS THE TEAM

ALL THE TEAM that compiled *Fulham's Golden Years* (above) is still going.

Ken has a new team at Ashwater Press, including Martin Plumb, Alan Williams, Derek the Frame and yours truly.

Professor Roodyn congratulates the authors on their tribute to Johnny Haynes. Right: Derek has framed Ken's black and whites, now he has to exhibit them.

Johnny Haynes – The Maestro was launched at the Cottage public house on 7th May. A meeting of old friends and a toast to an absent maestro. John Mitchell and Les Strong couldn't keep away, but behaved themselves.

Old Fulham. Good old Fulham celebrating back to the Cottage in these Premiership years.

John Mitchell and Les Strong supporting the launch of Johnny Haynes – The Maestro. *Two crowd pleasers from 1975, still pleasing the crowds in 2008. Two of them, two of us, but just one glass. Les must be drinking and John must be driving.*

YOU'RE HAVING A LAUGH!

"PREMIER LEAGUE – you're having a laugh!" is a taunt frequently heard since 2001 and entirely justified given Fulham's showing against Leyton Orient.

Supporters of Cheltenham, Lincoln and Bristol Rovers sang the same song with reason and with gusto.

Premier League – you're having a laugh. Yes and no. No, because all too often we are having a cry or a yawn or both. Perhaps Graham Taylor was right when he stated in 2001 that Fulham had (at best) three Premiership players. We were angry at the time as Saha, Boa, Finnan, Goma, John Collins and Maik Taylor were easily equal to the demands of the Premiership.

But we were wrong and the Turnip was right. Taylor and Tigana knew that the promotion squad needed strengthening, hence the addition of Van der Sar and Steed.

The Intertoto Cup was won with a talented team and Coleman took Fulham to a top ten finish in 2005 but he could not keep Finnan, Saha, Steed, Van der Sar or Boa. Nor could he replace such stars with proven players. Sanchez was given the money (more money than CC) but spent it in the lower leagues. His new recruits failed at the highest level. Baird, Boazza and Davis are the obvious examples.

For most of last season Fulham were without class and depended for survival on the return of Bullard and McBride, both strong characters and valiant warriors adored by the Fulham faithful and both well suited to relegation avoidance. Just what we needed but hardly likely to be scouted or touted by Chelsea or Liverpool. Clearly they lacked the artistry of JT's elan/flair/brio players. Sir Alex did not chase them, nor did Wenger. Bullard and McBride got fit again but not fit for purpose at Old Trafford or the Emirates.

Premier league – you're having a laugh? After seven seasons in the Premiership we have had precious few laughs. Premiership years, Premiership tears, grey days, grim days – grinding out a home win or hanging on for a precious away point. Keegan in 1999 and Tigana in 2001 took titles with 101 points. In the Premiership the likes of Fulham, Bolton, Wigan, Middlesbrough and Sunderland regard 40 points as job done, safe and sound for another season. But, another season of what? Relegation avoidance.

Welcome back to WBA, who have been up and down, up and down. Hello, Hull. How many Premiership players on your books? In Turnipspeak: "Not a lot." Last season Derby demonstrated the perils of promotion. Fulham survived again and the last three games of the season were far from dull, but the team

entertained (in the Keegan/Tigana sense of the word) just once in 2007–08 and just twice in 2006–07. How many of the squad are playing with a smile? Bullard.

Which members of the 2002 side played with a smile – Hayles and Boa? Where are the cavaliers and the comedians of yesteryear? Tosh, Keetch, Rodney Marsh, Les Strong, John Mitchell, George Best and Ivor Davies (pictured here)? Long gone. Ichabod, Ichabod, the glory and the beauty have departed, so it was business as usual in August 2008. Relegation avoidance at best but what is the alternative?

Business as usual in the Premiership or show business in the Coca Cola Championship? Coca Cola. Oh, yes – 'It's the real thing!' But is it?

My friend at Portman Road tells me that the Championship is less than entertaining and the overall standard is unimpressive. (Not bursting with Tigana teams.) Thus if the Premiership bottom six are grim then most Championship teams and most Championship matches are grim and grimmer.

Leeds and Leicester are bigger clubs than Fulham and more successful at the highest level. Leeds took the title in 1992 and O'Neill's Leicester won the

League Cup, but having fallen into the Championship they both fell out of it and down, down into the third division/league one.

In 1968 Fulham were relegated and it took 33 years to struggle up from 91st place. The lessons of Leeds and Leicester are not lost on Fulham fans. Premiership – you're having a laugh! Laughing all the way to the bank. Dempsey's goal against Liverpool was worth £28 million in 2007. What price the Murphy header at Portsmouth? £40 million?

Fulham struggled 2001 to 2008 and may struggle again this season. Hearty laughter? Perhaps not but we can endure the football while jumping for joy at the sight of a refurbished Craven Cottage. The beautiful game? Not much of that since Tigana, but the beautiful ground? Oh, yes! Yes indeed. Thank you, chairman.

Premiership – you're having a larf!

ONLY THE LONELY?

DEPICTED HERE are followers of Fulham who lasted the course. Followers of Fulham home and away from 1951 to 2001 and in some cases even longer.

The *Evening Standard* called us 'only the lonely' in February 1996 but back in the 1940s when John Humphris first visited Craven Cottage another voice used very different words in praise of 'the few'. Our prime minister, Winston Churchill, honoured the few, and his tribute can be reworked to honour the precious few who founded and funded Fulham 2000. Songs of praise also for the volunteers who launched *Cottage Pie* and did all the dirty work for the supporters' club.

You will recognise their faces even if you don't know their names. Amidst all the celebrations of 1999 and 2001 'New Fulham' should recognise the debt to the lonely and the few who worked so hard during that difficult decade 1986–1996. Without that creative minority, there would be little enough to celebrate as Fulham Park Rangers or ground sharing with Kingstonians. "So much owed by so many to so few."

These are veterans of the Clay, Bulstode, Marler crisis and the Fulham 2000 campaign. They were at the Cottage for that Scunthorpe fixture in January 1996 when a crowd of 2,176 ('crowd' as a euphemism here) watched Fulham. Fulham losing 3–1. Defeated and demoralised.

They were at Lincoln when even Simon Morgan gave up at 4–0 down in the ice and snow. They were at Torquay 'looking into the Conference.' For them Mansfield was magic in 1997 and Cambridge was a carnival in May.

The Premiership years mean much to the lonely and I saw most of them (now not so lonely) at Fratton Park in May 2008. Still going strong? Still going, certainly, but some of us are stronger than others while the famous four (Mary, Alex, Jim and Sammy) are watching from J block with Cyril Swain and Colonel Shrimpton.

For the lonely of 1986–1996 these Premiership years have been a haze and a daze. Thirty-three years awaiting a return to the top table. For many of us these Premiership days have been a crazy bonus. We did not want relegation with Sanchez but in our heart of hearts we know that relegation matters less than BTTC and home sweet home. In answer to that *Toofif* question: "Cottage or Premiership?" we all answer "Cottage." My grandson Max has known nothing but three promotions and the Premiership years. He and his friends might answer "Premiership," and he might concentrate on his rowing if/when we are relegated. Hundreds of junior season ticket holders might have drifted away if Fulham had lost those crunch away games at Reading, Man City and Portsmouth. I suspect that a Leeds, Leicester, Nottm Forest double relegation experience would see our gates slumping to 9,000. Hardly 'only the lonely' but probably commercially unviable and unacceptable to our chairman.

Certainly a repeat of 1986–87 would prove beyond the reach of the Muddymans and the Fulham 2000 campaigners. We saved Fulham then but we are too old, too tired and too poor to do so again.

In the middle of the muddle that was Fulham Park Rangers I stood with Dominic Guard at the Hammersmith End listening to the moans and the groans. "Memories, memories; all we are left with now are memories!" Dominic's comment then lives with me now. He turned his back on Fulham before the Premiership years. He was true to the Adams family and the spirit of '97. Not for him the Intertoto tour and the UEFA Cup. Not for him victory at Old Trafford. The mighty Magee is another who fought the good fight in the 80s and 90s but walked away from the Premiership. Brian Gee (left) refused to go to Loftus Road and remains in exile at Twickenham

Doncaster away 1997 – less lonely now.

collating old programmes. He remains in touch by telephone but it is the Oval rather than the Cottage in May and August. My own wife has mixed emotions about these Premiership years. Home and away with Branfoot, Adams, KK, JT, she cooled off at Loftus Road and cut down once we were safely back home in 2004.

Sheila loved Bologna, Split and Zagreb and she was at Stamford Bridge for the Boa goal in April 2003. She was at Boston for the League Cup fixture in September 2004 but she has handed her season ticket to a.n.other member of the family (the Fulham family) and prefers to suffer in silence at home with Jeff Stelling. On my return after a match the question is "Tea? Lemon and ginger or builder's brew?" She will have recorded all the relevant results and the league tables will have been updated. Fulham's goals will have been taped along with the CC or Sanchez or Hodgson interviews. Who could ask for anything more on returning home from Fulham 1 Sunderland 3 or Fulham 2 Birmingham 0?

Sheila was at Derby in May 1983 (pitch invasion, match abandoned, paradise postponed), and she was at Cambridge in May 1997 for the promotion party. Together we have made many trips to Portsmouth but she was not at Fratton Park this May. That ordeal was delegated to a most excellent son-in-law, Piers. Sufficient unto Sheila the agony and the ecstasy of watching and waiting with Lizzie. Once upon a time it was *Listen with Mother,* now it is listen with daughter.

Even Ken Coton, who recorded all the ups and downs, all the downs and ups 1961 to 2002, has eased off in the Premiership. The late night return to

Ashwater House, the threat of rain, hailstones, falling branches in Bishop's Park or those dreaded leaves on the line at Whitton... All too easy for Ken and his Whitton compatriot Robert to celebrate in front of Sky or join Alan Williams if the match is on Setanta.

Once it was "Ken, Ken, did you get the goal?" Ken would answer "I hope so. See Saturday's programme!" Please turn to all those golden goals in *Fulham's Golden Years*. Alternatively look at *Fulham Photos* for the Premiership years. If you want the striker striking *and* the ball entering the net, Ken is your man.

That was Ken at second division Hull in 1975. What about Premiership Hull in August 2008? Is Ken preparing his camera for all those Premiership games and all those Premiership goals? No, for a number of reasons, no. Ken says, "The world has changed!"

Freddie Fulham says, "Thanks, Ken; thanks for all those wondrous images of all those golden years."

Home and away for many a day. Riversiders to the left. Hammersmith Enders to the right.

POWERED BY PASSION

TOOFIF. Powered by passionate people from Toofif Towers who for 100-plus issues have campaigned for FFC and the ordinary fans. Extraordinary passion sustained over some difficult years and some difficult issues. In the darkest days the ground was at risk and yet another relegation seemed inevitable but *Toofif* found the answer with that cover of covers "We can still make the play-offs!"

Gallows humour, plus strong and constructive words from David Lloyd and team. Wit and wisdom from them and a long list of distinguished guests:

My name is David Lloyd and I captain the Fulham team. Our chosen topics this evening are pop music from the swinging Sixties and England's World Cup team of 1966 – and here are our resident experts David Hamilton and George Cohen.

Martin Plumb, Alex White, Jim Sims, Alex Ferguson and Michael Heatley. Random recollections from Cliffie orchestrated the celebration of better times with the Adams family, KK, JT and CC. Crucially there have been campaigns to save Craven Cottage and special issues for special people – remember the Simon Morgan Testimonial *Toofif* or issue 53 with 20p from each sale going to the Diana Memorial Fund.

4-4-2, Chris! 4-2-4, Chris! Both get you there – unlike the 4-5-1. 4-5-1 gets you nowhere. 4-5-1 is a Sanchez of a system.

Balloons, lampoons, cartoons – here a larf, there a larf – but also some serious purpose. Just one example (above) to demonstrate the economy and artistry of *Toofif* at its brilliant best. It works on the cover and it works on the pitch. CC took the point and the points – Fulham 3 Pompey 1 – when CC went 4-4-2 as advised by the Vatican via David Lloyd. (Remember Pope John Paul II? The only Pope to play in goal for FFC. A Hammy-ender during his student days in SW19 – from Green Pole to Purple Pontiff.)

Many old Fulham moaners have complained that the successes of 1997–2001 and the bright lights of the Premiership came at a price. Too high a price for the old guard (particularly Dominic Guard) – "It's not our club any more." Perhaps not, but thanks to *Toofif* the fans have a fanzine powered by passion, an informed and informative means of communication keeping us in touch with *our* club and in touch with each other.

Freddie Fulham says: "Nice one, David; nice one, son; nice one, David, let's 'ave another one."

Thanks to all those at Toofif Towers. Please keep up the good work.

DERBY DAYS AND DERBY NIGHTS

DERBY DAYS – 'bad'. Derby nights – 'good'.

A Derby day cost us the cup, the big one, the Watney Cup, in August 1970. Another Derby day cost us promotion in May 1983.

Derby days have been bad at Pride Park; they were worse at the old Baseball Ground. The very worst of many such bad Derby days was May 1983. Read all about the Baseball Ground in David Peace's *The Damned United*. Effing awful Derby in 1967, but effing good Derby promoted in 1959, and effing champions in 1972. Effing good, that Cloughie.

The ground may have been fit for baseball when it opened in 1889 but it was unfit for football by the 1990s, hence the move to Pride Park. The Baseball

Ground combined a difficult surface and a difficult atmosphere in 1983. Just how difficult we sensed at the time (caged below ground level) with viewing restricted by police horses. Not that those police horses were much use when the Derby fans kicked down the advertising hoardings and encroached on the pitch.

It looked bad at the time and this very summer I saw just how bad it all was when the entire match was shown again on *Match of the Day – Revisited*. At the time Super Mac and others protested to the referee and to the football authorities. The invasion of the pitch and the intimidation of players was evident in 1983. The injuries inflicted on Hopkins and Wilson were documented on the day. The match was 'abandoned' but soon brushed under a carpet at FA headquarters. Action in the courts never satisfied the manager. A token fine was too little and too late to bother Derby. Any such incident these days would be dealt with swiftly. Points deducted, many points deducted. Leeds, Luton and other clubs have been punished far more severely than Derby. Derby should have been relegated and Fulham awarded the points or at the very least offered a replay on a neutral ground within a week of the 'abandoned' match.

Perhaps Leicester would still have secured the promotion we longed for but the failure of Derby to control their crowd or protect our players warranted Draconian measures, not "Tut, tut; naughty, naughty; have a pale yellow card and a token fine." The recent televised showing of the fixture made the whole affair even worse than it seemed at the time. Injustice done and seen to be done. Justice not done and seen to be undone. Sorry – end of rant. Back to Pride Park.

Pride Park is one of the very best of the new grounds. Easy of access by rail with its own station and its own brewery. Excellent under-soil heating enabled us to play there on the frostiest of nights, in the bleakest of midwinter. Having warmed up at The Brunswick and having skated our way through the car park we endured a long old, cold old struggle but went home with all the points thanks to a late, late Carbonari own goal. Fortunate Fulham move out of the relegation places. Unlucky Derby – Poom in goal and doom in sight. They escaped relegation in 1983 but there was no escape in 2002 and 2008.

That was a good Derby night at Pride Park, an even better Derby night came to the Cottage in November 2000. Five good goals with the best in injury time from Saha. Fulham 3 Derby 2. That was in the League Cup as JT's Championship Fulham disposed of Premiership Derby. It was Premiership Fulham in January 2005 playing Championship Derby in the FA Cup. Being a day game it was unsurprisingly bad with Derby much the sharper side, playing much the sharper football. Somehow we caught up through Collins John – 1–1. Replay back at the Cottage where CC was far from happy with his 'mute' Riversiders. They were mute because they could see the poverty of Fulham's performance. Again (being a Derby day) it went badly, until extra time when ten-man opponents finally subsided. Fulham 4 Derby 2.

More inevitably bad Derby days last season. A yawningly modest performance at home ended 0–0 with yet more frustration on return to Pride Park. Fulham fans had long booked this as the can-win, must-win, first away win. They watch and wait. 0–1, 1–1, 2–1. "Told you so. Here we go." "Oh, no, and oh, woe!" Derby score and it's 2–2. Fulhamish very. Another late lead lost. Another away option wasted and another bad, bad Derby day.

Paul Pesch (the fox in the box) scores for Fulham against Wrexham in April 1999. He returned to the Cottage to score for Derby in the FA Cup in January 2005.

– 87 –

GOING, GOING, GONE

AFTER SUNDERLAND we were down, very down. We had all counted on a point or three, but dire in defence we gave them the game. Healy's well struck goal could have, should have, prompted a fight back, but yet more defensive howlers condemned us to defeat and another week in the relegation zone. "Down with the Derby, you're going down with the Derby!" So sang Sunderland and so sobbed all of us.

Going, going, gone to Manchester City – many supporters there but I of little faith was gazing at Craven Cottage from Barn Elms. With one hand on the bicycle and the other on the wireless, I was following the Fulham from afar while watching the final of the Hammersmith Regatta. Grandson Max was losing his race, Fulham were two goals down to Man City and Birmingham were beating Liverpool. Fulham were due to be relegated come 5pm…

As the race on the river continued, Liverpool scored twice to make it 2–2 with Birmingham in the Five Live commentary game. That report was suddenly interrupted by goal news – Man City 2 Fulham 1. Next came a shout of penalty

Max is a dedicated oarsman and has trained hard with his school VIII. School coach Mr West is a Cambridge blue. Max would love to follow West and Waller (below) to Cambridge. Ample room on this bench for Max.

at Eastlands. "Penalty saved!" but Murphy followed up to make it 2–2. Great fight back and yet it might not be enough.

Cycling faster and faster (with heart pounding) as Max and his crew approach Hammersmith Bridge. Still all square 2–2 at Birmingham when the commentators cross to Man City for injury time and Kama's goal. From two down to one up in 20 minutes. Going, going, gone…mad.

Gone crazy, gone berserk on a bicycle. Faster and faster now to join the rest of the family who are shouting for Max and for Fulham. Photo finish at Hammersmith, with Max and his crew declared the winners.

Proud parents go back to the boathouse for photographs of the medal ceremony. Proud grandparents cycle home slowly, very slowly. What a lovely view, what a lovely evening – time for a poem? "O frabjous day, callooh, callay! He chortled in his joy." (That Lewis Carroll may have been an Oxford man but he had a way with words.) Frabjous indeed this particular day.

Going, going, gone…to phone a friend. Phone a friend, or two or three or four or five (Fulham friends). Perhaps some champagne with Sheila now? Why not? Cheers! Delicious anticipation of those goals on *Match of the Day*.

THREE FULHAM FAMILIES

ONE: Pride of place goes to the Humphris household (1946–2008). In this chapter are the words of Derek's father, his brother and his nephew. Derek's own story is writ large thoughout all four volumes of *Following The Fulham*.

THE HOUSE THAT JACK BUILT

JACK TELLS HIS STORY

From the depths of rural Oxfordshire to my first match at Craven Cottage, collecting a dose of lead from a German machine gunner on the way. This was my situation on becoming an FFC supporter in January 1946 after five months in hospital and a posting to Hyde Park Barracks.

Joe Bacuzzi was one of my favourite players from the early days. However, after many years of some success, but many failures, we watched on the Swansea terraces as Fulham dropped to the basement of the Football League.

It became even worse until Mickey Adams achieved a much needed promotion.

The arrival of Mr Al Fayed was a fairy tale come true, as he was putting funds into Fulham rather than trying to extract property value. He forecast promotion to the Premier League in five years, which nobody believed. We were wrong. He did it in four, and the establishment and media have never forgiven him.

The 2007–08 season should have produced another relegation, but we lived on to fight again in the true Fulhamish spirit.

"HERE COME THE VULTURES..."

In the early Nineties, long cold afternoons in a largely empty Riverside Stand had made me question why I continued attending the ritual humiliation of match day. Results rarely went our way and the depths to which we were sinking was reflected in the number of seats removed that week to save maintenance costs.

A small advert in the matchday programme asked for reasonably fit volunteers to act as stretcher bearers; it sounded interesting with the bonus of free entry to the game. I think it was an evening game versus Doncaster Rovers when Declan (the only other volunteer) and I made our debut. Fair to say that the operation in those days was not as slick as it is now. We were still walking around pitchside to our seats when we were signalled on to treat an injured player. Little instruction or pack-drill but the job was done.

Over the years the regularity with which players have been stretchered off has decreased whilst their value has increased. In the early years Simon Morgan was by far our most regular customer. There have been many surreal moments, not least one warm day when Michael Jackson wandered by the dugout complete with parasol.

The chant of where were you when we were skint was an all-time classic. Working with Pierre Luigi Collina during an Intertoto Cup match was great – a top referee and a gentleman.

The need to be impartial is sometimes tested, as when carrying a Cambridge player off behind the Putney End goal as Mick Conroy buried a shot into the corner of the net. Being offered Damien Duff's shirt after the Chelsea doctor had cut it off to treat his dislocated shoulder – well, professional pride demanded a polite refusal.

Reaching the Premiership inevitably saw many changes and improvements throughout the club. Although the stretcher bearers were largely unaffected by these, we were required to sign away our broadcast image rights, ironically in the same week that David Beckham had done the same in return for thousands of pounds a week at Manchester United.

Later years have had their moments – getting caught between the man in the green underpants and the Chelsea masses was interesting. I was only too happy to follow the advice of the security guard – "Run for it." Besides the friendly banter that emanated from the old enclosure, there is only one negative

aspect to life as a vulture – no pre-match beer.

DANIEL'S DILEMMA

Despite the best efforts of his Fulham family, Daniel succumbed to peer pressure and took to supporting his local team, Crystal Palace, in his early years. Work commitments meant no football for a number of years before a change of job made Saturdays available again in 2006. Daniel was at Newcastle when Fulham won the match but lost Bullard. A return to match action at Craven Cottage promised much, but for most of the season delivered little. The pain of actively supporting Fulham was ultimately off-set by the euphoria of the greatest escape at Portsmouth.

CLOSE TO HOME

MY NAME is Olivier Butler. Let me introduce my parents – Piers and Lizzie Butler. They are enjoying the sunshine at the Hammersmith End on Boxing Day 1989 (below). My granny Sheila is with them and my grandfather Peter is

taking the photo. I am soon to be born in Paris.

Now you can see me wrapped up in an extra large Fulham scarf for my first visit to Craven Cottage in October 1992 (below). My grandparents took me to watch Fulham play Hull. We were not so happy in the enclosure as we watched Fulham go three goals down after twelve minutes. My granddad was not amused and words were spoken. The second half was more like it, with a final score of 3–3. Udo, Udo, Udo Onwere!

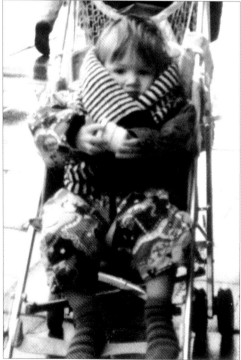

It was a temporary respite. A couple of years on and it is the spring of 1994 and I am contemplating Fulham's fortunes and misfortunes. My cousins from Derby haven't a care in the world. My grandmother went with them to Pride Park to watch the Rams beat Man City 5–1, but FFC are worse than the Yeovil. It's sad but true – Yeovil 1 Fulham 0 in the FA Cup with worse to come in the league. Swansea 2 Fulham 1 on May 7th 1994 and we're relegated. The fourth division awaits us.

Cheer up! Let's play happy families in 2001. Happy Riversiders in 2001. YES to promotion, YES to the Premiership and YES to a refurbished Craven Cottage. My father and my grandmother smile along with me but where is my grandfather? Taking the photograph! It can't be a Ken – it lacks the sharpness of a Ken.

May 2002 and that's a proper photo (below). Ken's camera depicts three generations of the family. Not me this time but my brother Max who has taken my seat and my season ticket. I did not go to Loftus Road where Max saw Fulham beat Liverpool. Indeed Max has been to Old Trafford and back with FFC. He saw Fulham beat Chelsea and Arsenal in 2006. What the Butlers saw here, what the Butlers saw there… but only one Butler saw Fulham come back from three goals down to Hull. Udo, Udo, Udo Onwere!

LOST AND FOUND

Pictured here is Major Findlay Thomson with PFT in about 1940. *PFT takes up the story in 1945.*

Findlay had been promoted to Lt Colonel but I remember him as the galloping major – always riding in and out of the family home. When present he disapproved of football in general and Fulham in particular. He disappeared for six or seven years in 1952 but then turned up in my Cambridge rooms with a new wife and a new child. No mention of Fulham there but many hints that I should seek employment at a boarding school well away from SW6. The major himself continued to gallop around the home counties, Abbot's Ride, Castle Royal, Farnham being the well chosen address for some of Fulham's first division years.

Communication was difficult as birthday cards and Christmas cards were returned by step-mother Irene. Eventually my sister Judi (based in Canada) managed to Google up the major's time and place of death. That seemed to be that until July 2008 when Judi was staying with me in Mortlake and undertook further research in person. Deep in the west country she found her step-sister who talked of the major's belated conversion to FFC – Damascus Road, Dawlish?

While some of us were out in the wind and rain following the Fulham to Exeter, Torquay and Plymouth, my father was sitting in the warmth of his Torbay home listening to the results and preparing to join Jimmy Hill for *Match of the Day.*

Thus as the Cambridgeshire Thomsons turn their backs on Fulham and become more and more devoted to Chelsea there is comfort and consolation in the return to Craven Cottage of Ian (the prodigal son) plus now the posthumous stabling of the galloping major.

Merula giveth thanks: "There is more joy in J block over one sinner that repenteth than over ninety and nine just Riversiders which needeth no repentance."

Olivier and Max jumping for joy in May 2001 at the end of the season of seasons.

FULHAM FAMILY IN HAMBURG

WE HAVE Kevin Keegan to thank for the Hamburg link. KK was their super star 1977–80, hence their interest in Fulham from 1997. Hamburg supporters came to Craven Cottage to watch the rise and rise of KK's FFC. Fulham supporters made their way to Hamburg to learn more about their manager's former glory. Thus in 1998 Derek met up with Björn.

Björn and friends, just back from the beaches of Croatia.

Björn celebrated this friendship in a recent email:

To Fulham Derek: Today 10 years ago we met – a long time with a lot of good memories. Here are just a few. Asking you for a Fulham scarf; having a first chat despite my limited English during a match with Altona; FA Cup for Fulham at Old Trafford with a signed picture of Craven Cottage; celebrating your promotion in 1999; Berlin and Cottbus with fireworks; Fulham win 3-0 at Spurs; Fulham in Berlin for the UEFA Cup; Springsteen concerts celebrating your birthday; a day out at Torquay with Fulham – "Near Brighton?"; 6–0 win at Rostock; meeting some Geordies with you; New Year's Eve in London; a lot of other memorable days and nights; and finally another Springsteen concert in Hamburg.

This has become a real, deep friendship. Looking forward to the next ten years – hope to see you again soon. We watch Fulham at Everton and then maybe a good night out in Manchester.

Your friend Björn.

"Zwei Seelen und eine Gedanke, zwei Herzen und ein Schlag!" – FFC mit HSVH. Björn's friends have become supporters of FFC. Verena accompanied

The choristers of Hamburg.

Björn to Fulham's match with West Ham. Dirk met up with us at Molyneux for Wolves 2 Fulham 1. Oli and Björn were part of Fulham's UEFA challenge and provided our refreshments at the Olympic stadium in Berlin.

Derek, Steven, Alan and Karen have attended Hamburg fixtures. The fellowship of football has moved on into matters musical – "Auf Flügeln des Gesanges." The CAMRA members have extended their repertoire. "Ohne Hast, aber ohne Rast."

My own Hamburg links are regimental rather than recreational. Falling-bostal garrison rather than singing songs and terrace talk. Rugby with the Royal Tank regiment 1961–62 not football with Hamburg. There were visits to the beer cellars of Hamburg and Hanover but soldiers then tended to prefer quantity to quality. Oh Björn, oh Alan – we could have done with your advice. "Mehr Licht, mehr Licht!"

Björn's next visit is set for 31st October, the anniversary of our stay in Zagreb. (Dinamo 0 Ulham 3.) Björn back in Keegan's Liverpool where in

February 1975 Derek watched Fulham beat Everton. Time for a happy return to Goodison with a little help from Björn.

With a lot of help from Björn. "Ein feste Burg ist unser Björn, ein gute Wehr und Waffen."

Combined ops – the FFC Three and the Hamburg Two on their way to the Man City ground.

PALACE HOTEL
ZAGREB d.d.

AROUND THE GROUNDS

VIA ASHFORD AND the Arsenale to Bologna. Up the A1 for Boston. By train to Bournemouth and Brighton. Back to Ashford and the Arsenale for Croatia part one (Hajduk Split). Croatia part two was via Hanover to Zagreb for Dinamo 0 Ulham 3.

Via Ashford and the Arsenale again for Fiesole and the Viola before bread and butter fixtures at Cambridge, Chester and Colchester, Derby and Exeter, Fulham and Grimsby, Hereford and Ipswich.

Not so bread and butter – Singapore Airlines to Jerudong with Roy Dwight's nephew plus Beardsley and KK.

Via Luton to Kenilworth Road and up the A1 to Mansfield or the A11 to Norwich, the M4 to Oxford, the A1 to Peterborough, the 283 bus to QPR, the fast train to Reading, back to the A1 for Sheffield United via Mansfield.

Use the underground to Tottenham and to Underhill, long weekend at the Vetch, longer weekends at Mansfield for Wednesday and Wolves, some x-rated riots at Elland Road and the Baseball Ground, fast trains to York. And finally the Orient Express to Zagreb? Requested but just not possible in 2002 – autumn leaves on the line – so we flew via Hanover and returned to the slow boat in May 2003 – Putney Pier to Greenwich for Charlton at the Happy Valley.

Via Ashford and the Arsenale to Zagreb (2002) and Zamora (2008). An A to Z of following the Fulham with Sheila. My thanks to the best of companions at all these fixtures. Well, all but one. Sheila was there in Lincolnshire when Gazza turned out for the Pilgrims and FFC beat Boston 4–1 in September 2004. Part-time supporter PFT remained in detention at school.

From Ashford mud and Boston stump to Zagreb via Hanover and Bandar via Singapore.

SAMMY – 10th JULY 2008

HERE WE ARE down by the river at Mortlake, sitting in the garden of The Ship toasting you in London Pride and remembering you. Sammy the schoolboy at Emanuel. Sammy at Wembley in '75. Sammy travelling with Mary Doughty

then, Sammy travelling with Barbara Doughty now. The funeral was strictly private, attendance by invitation only. Barbara was not invited but she was there. Barbara was there for Mary and for Fulham and for you.

Others were waiting for you in the garden of remembrance. Many more were waiting at The Ship. Tales of Sammy in Munster Road, tea after the match with Ollwyn and Mick, drinking your tea and gazing at Sally and Jan and Di.

Following the Fulham home and away, developing a career as a taxman – Sammy the civil servant with the Inland Revenue and Sammy the civil servant with FFC. Sammy the Steward. At first for the pocket money but later as a senior steward at the Hammersmith End. Sammy the good steward, the good shepherd, attempting to look after youngsters who wanted to stand in or on the seats. Sammy the good steward, the good shepherd, looking after not so youngsters who wanted to gossip about Busby and Best, Mullery and Moore, Ivor and Big Jim Stannard.

Trips down memory lane to Cold Blow Lane, long weekends at Blackpool or Brighton or Southsea. Sammy, first one on the pitch for the Walsall sit-in; Sammy, last one off the pitch. SOS save our club 1986–87, SOS Fulham 2000, SOS back to the Cottage 2004. Sammy was always there. Black gloves on, black gloves off. In 1975 black hair, in 1985 black and white hair, in 1995 silver hair, in 2004 snow white hair, but back at the Cottage.

Sammy at Emanuel, wearing his prefect's badge.

Sammy we toasted you with pride in London Pride and when that ran out (as it did), we moved on to the guest ale Oakhill's Golden Goal.

Here's to you, Sammy! A few own goals but many more golden goals over the years and many a golden memory of Sammy the lad and Sammy the steward.

TALES FROM THE RIVERBANK

AN ESSAY IN honour of Martin Plumb and in memory of Cyril Swain – Martin very much with us, prolific chronicler of all things Fulham and most recently biographer of Johnny Haynes; Cyril Swain, one of the directors who saved Fulham from Marler Estates and the merger with QPR (Fulham Park Rangers).

The programme cover opposite captures the tension of those days. Terraces almost empty but the two or three gathered together still determined to make their point. "We'll never leave the Cottage!"

Thanks to Jimmy Hill, Tom Wilson, Bill Muddyman and Cyril Swain (left) the club was rescued and the ground saved. Just like that? No. It is a tortuous tale from the riverbank and one which Martin Plumb must tell. Dennis Turner has provided a masterly summary of the issues

Crowd: 3,798. Final score: Fulham 0 Port Vale 6.

1986–97. However, at Bill Muddyman's suggestion I have started working my way through the dozens of files in his family archives.

For the moment let this programme cover be witness to the enormity of the task facing Cyril Swain and his fellow directors. With crowds of 3,798 they had to take on the millions of pounds possessed by property magnates such as Marler, Cabra and the Royal Bank of Scotland. Very much David against Goliath. Enter just such a David. David Shrimpton (of the founding family, joining Cyril as a director) to the rescue in 1996–97. Just as Micky Adams dragged us away from relegation to the Conference so David Shrimpton helped Cyril and the Muddymans to save the ground from the goliaths of CPO and RBS.

Detailed explanation will follow in due course, but it was a narrow escape and there were awkward, painful, schismatic fallings-out within the board. At the eleventh hour (and the 59th minute of the eleventh hour) David found another Goliath. A giant of a white knight, a golden knight, Goliath the Good from Harrods. May 1997 – the month of a most improbable double for Fulham. FFC promoted for the first time in 16 years and FFC owning the ground for the first time in 101 years. Now that really was a double to stand comparison with anything achieved by Spurs or Arsenal or Man Utd.

Look again at that programme cover and note the message: "We'll never leave the Cottage!" We did, of course, and we were (albeit briefly) in exile at QPR but by then we were the Premiership big brothers and QPR were the much relegated poor relations.

Note also the score that day. Fulham 0 Port Vale 6. Fulham 0 (as in nil), Port Vale 6 (as in six). (Eight matches without a win assuring us of 20th place in the third division.) We have moved onwards and upwards since then.

A tale best told by Martin Plumb. A tale from the riverbank in which Cyril Swain must feature as one of the good guys. A good guy, a gentleman and a gentle man. Over to Freddie Fulham for the chorus: "Nice one, Cyril; nice one, son!"

Author Martin Plumb chats with adoring fans

DEAR BILL

THIS IS NOT Private Eye and this is not an attempt at satire. It is a belated attempt to thank friends and benefactors. Where would Fulham be without Bill and Andy Muddyman? Not at Craven Cottage and not in the Premiership. Bill and Andy are pictured above; Bill holds the championship medal awarded to Jean Tigana in May 2001.

Jimmy Hill headed up the 1987 to 1997 rescue operation but Bill and Andy provided the financial backing to carry us through those difficult years. Yes, Chairman Mo transformed Fulham's finances 1997–2008. Premiership ambitions from day one. Premiership achieved in style 2001. Premiership status defended 2001–08. Note however the major contribution of Bill and Andy to the early years of Mo's chairmanship. They remained as directors to represent Old Fulham and to defend the faith of the old believers.

I have been allowed access to the Muddyman archive (fascinatingly detailed documentation of 1986 to 2004). One day perhaps I might attempt a Dennis Turner of an appreciation of some of those papers but for the moment just a broad brush "thank you" letter to father and son. The Shrimptons founded the club and supported it through four generations. The Muddymans (with a little help from Fulham 2000) saved Fulham and Craven Cottage.

The angel is in the detail. (Devilling of that detail to follow in another volume.) Sufficient unto this volume, two anecdotes. Anecdote one from Bill's study where Jean Tigana's 2001 championship medal has pride of place. JT gave his medal to Bill as a mark of friendship and as proof positive of the Muddyman role in the making of our season of seasons.

The second tale comes from the Deva stadium, Chester. After a long, long day following the Fulham and a late, late session of tea and sympathy with Big Jim Stannard and Simon Morgan it was time to look for our beds. Many phone calls but no taxis. Nothing for it but to walk on through the wind and rain. After some hundred yards, a car pulled up beside us. Andy Muddyman to the rescue. Mr and Mrs Thomson were delivered to the doorstep of their hotel. And so to bed – an hour earlier and a deal warmer and dryer than the followers of the Fulham pictured below. Many and many the private kindnesses in addition to the main business – SOS FFC.

Dear Bill, dear Andy, thanks for everything.

CHOIR POWER

SOME SONGS we sing – a selection from the Hammersmith hymnal.

HYMNS ANCIENT

On the way to Wembley in 1975 we sang a number of songs: "Jimmy, Jimmy Conway, Jimmy Conway on the wing" or that song of praise for our very own academic number 5 (left): "Wingers small and wingers pacey, none of them get past John Lacy."

So much for the first nine matches of the FA Cup run but when it became clear that we might face West Ham in the final there was an urgent meeting of senior supporters. Jimmy Hill and Tosh were charged with sorting out a song for Wembley. The Hammers had *Bubbles* and we ended up with *Viva el Fulham*. Tosh and Jimmy Hill conducted choir practices on the pitch and we adopted this song with reservation. Many preferred *Down by the Riverside* but each January we announce that "*This* year we're going to win the Cup", sing *Viva el Fulham*, and each year we surrender to Hayes or Yeovil or Orient or Bristol Rovers. Gleefully Orient and Rovers sing back "Premiership? You're having a larf!" *Non sine causa.*

THE FULHAM SONG

As a reminder here are the words of Jimmy Hill's Fulham song to be sung to the tune "Old Father Thames".

Some teams may come,
Some teams may go.
Whatever their end
    may be,
But Fulham will still keep
    rolling along,
Right on to victory . . . . .

HYMNS MODERN

On the way to the Premiership it was "Ooh, ah, Tigana!" and "Al Fayed, Oh, ho, ho." These were genuine examples of creative writing at the Hammersmith End. Less original was *We are the Champions* – very true in 1999 and in 2001 – but this Queen anthem was seldom heard at Loftus Road. More appropriate to the

"We ARE Barcelona!" We are Mr and Mrs Ron Atkinson.

Loft and the mood of the fans was "We've got to get out of this place" and "Take me home."

From August 2004 club and ground have delighted in *Back Home*. Chairman Mo offered his own composition, *We're not Barcelona*, but later took the lead in person on the pitch. His recording of *Back Home* formed the musical prelude to the Bolton match of August 2004.

A SONG FOR EUROPE

In Athens the ancient architecture inspired the travelling fans. Time for our own vintage vinyl: "Jimmy, Jimmy Conway, Jimmy Conway on the wing". An old favourite from 1997 – "Who put the ball in the Carlisle net? Rodney, Rodney McAree!" – was reworked as "Who put the ball in the Athens net? Marlet, Marlet" and as for Athens so for Haka, Zagreb and Berlin. "Marlet, Marlet!"

At Sochaux there was a touch of *Toofif* about the hymn chosen for evensong. "You all support Switzerland, you all support Switzerland!" Many of our choristers had reached Sochaux via Geneva, hence the topical lyric. Come Bologna we adopted *Blue Moon* not in honour of Man City but because it was belted out by the town band in the main square. The locals were unsure of the words so the Traveller took over the baton. The perfect end to a perfect evening on and off the pitch.

On our way to Berlin we met up with some Man Utd fans who suggested a Mancunian ditty from their travels through Germany in the UEFA Cup and the Champions League. "Can we bomb you every week?" They had used this in Dresden and advocated it for Berlin. Fulham did *not* adopt that one. *Genug ist genug* was the comment at the time and also after the match when the FFC choir performed at the Hotel Adlon.

THE PREMIERSHIP HIT PARADE

Select a top ten. Start with five from the Green Pole album of songs for Fulham.

John Lennon's *Starting Over* for New Fulham.

Status Quo's *Rocking all over the World* for those veterans the Thamesbank travellers, especially Alex.

The Clash's *London Calling* for all who sit by the river.

Andy Williams's *You're just too Good to be True* when we win at home.

Tina Turner's *Simply the Best* for JT and Saha in 2001 or for manager Hodgson and captain McBride in 2008.

This selection ought to be made by our resident DJ and MC, David Hamilton. Advice aplenty from Fulham's very own singer/songwriters. (Ralph McTell, Clive Allen and Chris Guard plus, perhaps, Michael Jackson. Remember Wacko's walkabout? He joined Chairman Mo under a parasol. "And did those feet in ancient time walk upon Fulham's mountains green?")

We all enjoyed the FA Cup fixture with Stoke. We won 3–0 and we sang about Montella: "He comes from Italy, etc." Stoke responded with *Delilah*. We welcome Stoke to the Premiership and look forward to another singsong this season. Book now for 25th April. April showers for April choirs.

Liverpool and Celtic claim "Walk alone." Chelsea own *Blue is the Colour*, and Fulham respond with songs sacred and profane: "Stick the blue flag up your ****".

December brings seasonal sounds. Jingle, bells. "Oh what fun it is to see Fulham win away!" When did Fulham last win away at Christmas? Not 2005 or 2006 or 2007, but come December 2008 we will give it another go when we visit Tottenham.

"Skint" used to be popular with our visitors but for most of last season the inevitable chant was "Down with the Derby, you're going down with the Derby!" Indeed for most of that season we hummed away *sotto voce:* "We're not very good, we're not very good!"

There were louder outbursts in honour of Brian McBride and Jimmy Bullard, while Chairman Mo received regular endorsement: "He wants to be a Brit and QPR are ****." Meanwhile up in the Loft, QPR were singing those songs which question our paternity. They were preparing to roast us in 2008–09. At 4pm on 11th May, we might have started on "Not tonight, Josephine!" but at 5pm "Staying up, staying up!" was back at number one. It had been heard at Reading and Man City along with "Keep the faith."

Top of the pops for me last season was that happy clapper from 3rd May as Birmingham were outsung and outdone. "The Cottage began loud and became supersonic" – *Sunday Observer.* Thank you, LG, for the clappers. Mine is almost clapped out but I might ask Derek to frame it as a precious relic with

miraculous powers. All LG clappers were working overtime in J block that afternoon.

Thank you, Hammersmith Enders, for keeping the faith and singing out whatever the weather and whatever the score.

BEYOND OUR KEN or
OVER TO ORMONDROYD

AS THE *Cottagers' Journals* might well have phrased it: "Behold, Merula passed by Ken and cast his mantle upon Ormondroyd."

Elijah Merula wrote the FFC match reports for many years, Ken Coton was club photographer for many more. Now the mantle of Elijah Merula has fallen upon young Ormondroyd. We used to pay our old penny for Merula's verdict on Fulham v Leicester. Admission 4 pence. Then we looked at Ken's pictures from Fulham 2 Leicester 1 in November 1961. For the cup game with Leicester this season it is Ormondroyd who captures the passing scene. Catch his column on *volzy.com*.

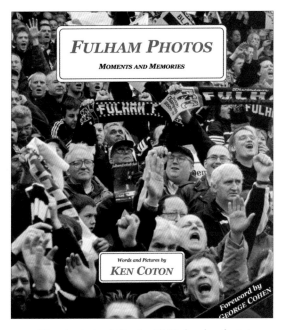

The jacket of Ken's 2002 book of pictures featured serendipitously the young Ormondroyd – holding banner at right.

Time was the match magazine looked after us. Time was Ken's goals were the main event in the programme. Now it is Elisha Ormondroyd who brightens up your screen with the passing scene. Tommy Trinder was right, we are such "lucky people" – thanks to Merula, Coton and Ormondroyd.

Programmes – never throw any away. I did. Big mistake. In 1984 I took some thirty years' worth of programmes to the Hammersmith End where they found good homes with Derek and Brian. Thus extra shelf space at home (Lebensraum) but, at times, a sense of loss and a lack of visual references. All change in 2002 when a kind old boy from the enclosure left me his collection dating back to the golden age of Ken. These programmes are stored at school and many the detention, exam, invigilation, prep period that has been enlivened by a rip-roaring read, a nostalgia-drenched trip down memory lane.

What has all this got do with the Premiership? Much, because in those days we had photos of the man, the ball, and the net. We had travel notes from Mary Doughty and match reports from Alex the Traveller plus a short sharp message from the manager: *Taking Stock*, *Ray Says*, *Brace Yourself.* Perhaps eight pages in total (that included the adverts) and all for about 6d.

Now we pay over £3 for too many adverts and too few goals. Bigger and better? Bigger certainly but less useful. What we want is Watney's. Watney's Red Barrel and Deans Blinds. Just one or two adverts. What we want is Ken or Ormondroyd with two or three goals and two or three passing scenes. Images which convey the atmosphere, the ambience of "Oh, you lucky people!" – our Craven Cottage, our river Thames and our Bishop's Park. It is all so image worthy. It is all so photogenic.

Ruskin Spear and Jason Bowyer have celebrated this passing scene – Fulham as fine art, with Ken and Ormondroyd extending the tradition. Ken's *Fulham Photos* took us up to 2004. Over to Ormondroyd for his albums of

images. Fulham's Premiership years plus his lavishly illustrated *Diary of a Johnny Come Lately*.

These are Ormondroyd's own words. "I am a man of Kent. A Kentish man and cricket fan who in 1995 fell for the Cottage and fell in with the crowd at the Hammersmith End." Not a bad time to sign up. Get Branfoot out, get Adams in, back from the brink, *On Song For Promotion* with Simon Morgan. Goodbye and thank you, Jimmy Hill; welcome, welcome, Chairman Mo! Going up with KK, going up with JT, leaving the Cottage, life in the Loft, BTTC, beating Man Utd at Old Trafford. Back home in 2004 – hooray! – relegation avoidance with CC; wow – beating Chelsea and the Arsenal in 2006. Life in the slow lane with Sanchez, life in the fast lane with Roy and Ray… swimming.

Now is the winter of our discontent made glorious summer by this son of Hodge, this Hodgson and this Lewington. Lest we forget, lest we forget – we log on or we tune our LG sets to this son of Ken (this grandson of Merula), this Ormondroyd.

A selection of Ormondroyd's evocative Fulham pictures. Ken's Coton's black-and-white photograph of Bishop's Park from 1961 (centre) complements the young master's own park picture.

A typical Ormondroyd special.

CONTINUITY MAN

WORDS OF WISDOM from Les Strong (FFC 1971–83, 424 appearances) – true friend of Fulham. 'One of us' as a player, as a chef, as a host on match days, and as one of those members of the Fulham family who always turn out when needed at Fulham related events.

Would any of your team have survived / flourished in the Premiership?

"Today's Premiership has many world class players, but also some very average players. I believe Lacy, Slough, Conway, Mitch, Barrett and myself could have played and survived today, as well as (and regardless of age) Mullery and Moore – for a couple of seasons at least."

Were we good enough to go up and stay up in '82–'83?

"We were definitely good enough in '82–'83. Peyton, Houghton, Davies and Parker were all top players. The hard part as always is getting there. With a few signings we could have stayed up."

How did we stay up in 2006–07 and 2007–08?

"Apart from maybe about eight teams the Premiership is average, and we were able to stay up because 12 teams were very beatable. No-one gave us a chance in the last six games (even myself, I admit!) but all the games were winnable, and it helped that Portsmouth were playing in the final the next Saturday. But still it was an incredible run and results, one that will go down in Fulhamish history."

Les turned up for Ken Coton's photographic exhibition evening and promptly entered into a funny face competition. Perhaps they were discussing memories of Les's exploits as a Fulham chef in 1986 (menu left).

ON THE ONE HAND...

MAY 2007 – On the one hand relief at victory over Liverpool (and the comfort of other results going our way). Safe at last. Relegation avoided.

On the other hand, anxiety at the prospect of another season without any of the flair players recruited by Tigana. Players who could pass, players who

could turn defence into attack, players who brought joy to the game and joy to the fans. The financial case for selling Saha, Finnan, Steed and Boa may have been strong but apart from Bullard we had not replaced quality with quality.

In addition, the money, the status, the schedules which go with the Premiership do not make up for the good old away days which were so much fun in 1997 and 1999 and 2001. The magic of Mansfield may have been the magic of the moment but Cambridge was fun as well as football.

The Championship contains several delightful watering holes – Ipswich, Norwich, Southampton, Colchester and Plymouth. There *is* life (the good life?) beyond the Premiership. Yes, relegation would have hurt but with two away wins in two seasons what is the incentive to 'Follow the Fulham' around the grounds?

OK, so I am a poor old thing with just four away days this season (Exeter, Portsmouth, Chelsea, Reading) but just think of the time, travel, money and pain saved by suffering it all on TV rather than in person.

In the golden days of '97 and '99 and 2001, or even in the darker days of stagnation and relegation, the pain could be eased by an overnight stay at Brighton or Grimsby or Swansea. The sea breeze might bring some ease as did good companions and fellow travellers. Of the Premiership at present only Portsmouth chimes: "Let's make a weekend of it – beside the seaside, beside the sea."

FULHAM'S PREMIERSHIP XI

IN GOAL – VDS. Simply the best; clean sheets at Anfield and Highbury; saved one penalty at Anfield and two in the Villa match; European cup winner's medals with Juventus, Man Utd and Fulham.

Back four – Volz, Goma, Hangeland and Rosenoir. Goma saved us again and again at Loftus road. A superb reader of the game (and a charming chap) Hangeland helped steady matters at the eleventh hour in April and May 2008. Can time a tackle and is good on the ball. Volz was excellent at the back at Loftus Road and saved CC during an injury crisis by taking up an attacking midfield position. His goal at Chelsea endeared him to Fulham fans. His journalism in a foreign land and a foreign tongue impressed many supporters of other clubs. Rosenior may not have been the best of our Premiership defenders or the most accurate crosser of the ball but as Leroy's son he had an understanding of 'old Fulham' and gave wholehearted performances. Rufus B and Liam were not as talented as Finnan but seemed warmer characters. A smile on the face and a bit of banter.

Midfielders – Steed, Sean Davis, Bullard and Boa. Steed and Davis could make tackles, win the ball and carry it forward, plus their goals in key games saved us from relegation (Steed away at Leeds in 2002 and Davis at home to Charlton). Boa began with a smile but lost it as captain. Yes, he lost it in several senses but he could single-handedly turn a game as he did against Liverpool in 2006. Plus – and a big plus – "Who put the ball in the Chelsea net? Boa, Boa!" Yes, twice – once at Stamford Bridge and once at Craven Cottage. Fulham 1 Chelsea 0, March 2006. Thanks, Boa, but you do not retain the captaincy.

Perhaps Jimmy Bullard should be captain as he talks the talk, walks the walk and runs the run. Fulham's action man, yet a wonderful dead-ball specialist. Won hearts with his early goals, retained hearts by his PR work while injured, fired the recovery under Hodgson. Made the goals which saved us from relegation. Is as popular at Fulham as he was at Wigan. According to the Hammersmith Enders, he is better than Gerrard and Lampard. Perhaps not as a passer of the ball but he is a much loved and colourful character. Another Tosh, or Ooh, Rodney, Rodney, or Les Strong. An Ivor of a personality, one of us.

Up front, leading the line – Saha and McBride. Saha was incomparably the best striker in the league in 2000–01 and he started his Premiership career with two brilliant goals at Old Trafford. Sir Alex took notice and hunted him

Saha scores again! Fulham 3 WBA 0, February 2003.
Right: Maik Taylor, Mr Dependable on the bench.

down. Much missed by CC but the money was good and Saha's injuries while at Man Utd may mean that we had the best of the bargain. Saha's first touch, power in the air and ability to score with either foot made him the most exciting leader of the line since Ivor. Thus far in the Premiership no Fulham forward has matched his skill and athleticism. Brian McBride was a very different player. Target man, good in attack and defence, he lacked the pace of a Boa or a Kamara but scored many a brave, brave headed goal. His injury so early last season caused major problems on and off the pitch. His return made a fight-back possible – and how the crowd loved him! He shed as much blood for Fulham as Roger Brown and he had the same guts and go. Leadership by example. Ray Lewington confirms the importance of Captain Courageous to Fulham's return from the brink. A devout man, a family man and one of those players who restore one's faith in football and in the USA.

On the bench? Over to you. Please consider Maik Taylor, Rufus Brevett, Lee Clark and Bazza. Not necessarily the best of the rest but 'characters' who had much to offer Fulham and the Premiership.

ONE OF US

LES STRONG, John Mitchell, Tony Gale, Ivor – they are 'of us' in the sense that they remain fond of Fulham, and true to FFC in bad times as well as good.

Mary Doughty's funeral – a bad time graced by the kind words of Tony Gale; the launch of Real San Paulo (a local junior XI) – a good time made better by Ivor's letters of encouragement and acceptance of hon life presidency; the exhibition of Fulham photos at the Riverside Studios – graced, of course, by Ivor but further lifted, enlivened, entertained by Mr and Mrs Terry Angus.

The Johnny Haynes book evening at The Cottage was a well organised affair with an excellent slide show. It became more, much more, than memory lane when Les Strong and John Mitchell added their anecdotes to the archives. One of us, two of us, back with us for the fun of it.

Terry Angus endeared himself to all Fulham fans by joining us in the crowd at Brisbane Road in March 1997. In an outsize Fulham wig, Terry took the baton to conduct the singing of "Going up, going up, going up!" One of us in word, one of us in deed, one of us indeed. Terry returned to recall those days at David Roodyn's lunch club. Hilarious the occasion and tall the Terry, almost as tall as some of his stories.

Mr Fulham in the crisis years was Simon Morgan and he remained with FFC as Mr Community. Some 20 years of service, distinguished service, well summed up by Dennis Turner's tribute. Put less formally by Bobby Box, Ray Brookes, in a pre-match gossip by the river,

Mr and Mrs Terry Angus happily supported the Back To The Cottage campaign.

"Morgs is one of us and the last Fulham player to be so termed; the present lot aren't ours on and off the pitch." Much nodding and "More's the pity"-ing and "Those were the days"-ing, as we shuffled off to our seats.

Simon Morgan (right) has a very special place in the fight for survival 1987–97 and in the Premiership years of 2001–2008 but is he the last 'one of us'? Perhaps not because who was that in the crowd away at West Ham in the very worst of the relegation dogfight? Brian McBride with his lovely wife. Captain Courageous on the pitch, Captain Magnanimous off the pitch. A man for all seasons, no fair-weather friend. His goals gave us hope in April 2008, his leadership was essential to the great escape in May. Player of the Season twice. Now absent friend but like Graham Leggat still with us despite the Atlantic. Still one of us – or as Freddie Fulham says "Lovely man with lovely wife!"

One of us and another of us, in among us at West Ham.

KEEPING THE FAITH

MANAGERS AND COACHES must motivate their players and the fans, but there are times when they blink and blank. (Turnip talk, Hoddlesque ramblings,

RAY WRITES...

Warnock ranting.) Sanchez assured the press, if not the Fulham fans, that he could have, would have, saved Fulham from relegation. Turnip talk? Hoddlesque? Warnocking?

For a more realistic analysis of how it was done, I asked Ray Lewington about the low points of 2007–08.

He said: *I think the lowest I felt last year was after the Sunderland home match. Having played well earlier in the season at the Stadium of Light, we were confident we could win well. It turned into a disaster, and I think most people felt our last chance of survival had disappeared.*

A supplementary question concerned the loss of McBride for so much of the season.

When Brian McBride's injury was diagnosed and we were told that he would miss a good chunk of the season, we lost lots of different things. Obviously firstly we lost a very good player, one who we could rely on to score his fair share of goals; we also lost the only player of his type in the squad. We also lost our captain. A player who on and off the field led by example whom both staff and players respected. It's impossible to quantify his worth to us in terms of points, but we all know how much we missed, and are going to miss, this fantastic pro.

How important was Bullard's return to fitness?

What can we say about Jim? A magnificent character on and off the pitch, he pumped new life into us when he returned and undoubtedly played a major part in our survival. As he gets stronger he will get better, and it will be lovely to have him in at the start of the new season.

Did the fans make a difference in April/May 2008?

Our support home and away never waned even when the odds looked against us. It was a team thing. If the players had lost faith that we would survive we would have gone down, and if the supporters had lost faith in the team we would certainly have gone down. Of that I'm sure.

And what about Roy Hodgson?

Roy never lost his nerve going into the last games; he still preached the same things as when he first arrived. He and Mike Kelly deserve so much of the credit. I'm very lucky that I was part of this season which will go down in history as the 'Great Escape'.

Roy Hodgson, fid def. As a defender of the faith, he is generosity and gravitas personified.

Roy and Ray – as keepers of the faith, they are exemplary.

Right: Ray Lewington, cover star. Below: 'The Don' welcomes Ray back to Plough Lane. Below right: the Sanchez system – 4-5-1, with Sanchez scoring (but not against Fulham, and certainly not with Fulham).

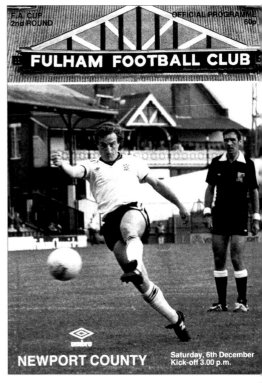

This evening it is our pleasure to welcome to Plough Lane our nearest Football League neighbours, Fulham F.C., with a special hello to one of our former players Ray Lewington.
Tonight will be our fourth meeting in the League with Fulham and hopefully we can celebrate our

NOT ONLY BUT ALSO

NOT ONLY FULHAM favourite Ivor Davies, but also highly regarded player and player-manager Ray Lewington. Together on the pitch under Super Mac in 1981–83 and together again as shown in this programme cover in more difficult times 1986–91.

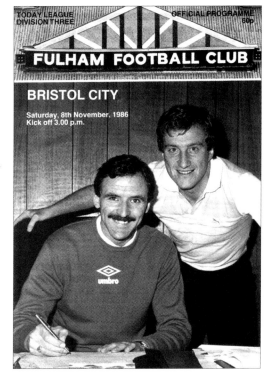

Ivor never made it into the Premiership but remains a regular visitor, match-day host and programme commentator. Ray returned in July 2004 to open the refurbished Craven Cottage. As manager of Watford he wrote of the difference between the traffic cones in Bishop's Park and the delights on offer at the Motspur Park training ground. Come the relegation struggles of 2006–08 he returned to FFC. "It's nice to be back home again."

Nice to see you, Ray, and thanks for 28 years of devoted service to all things Fulham.

Ray joined Fulham from Wimbledon via Vancouver Whitecaps in 1980 but he was already known to Fulham from his days as a playmaking midfielder at Chelsea. He was first sighted on Good Friday 1977 – Ray was flying that day. An early take-off as Peter Storey kicked him into the air. He kicked Ray's ankle on the way up and he kicked Ray's ear on the way down. GBH, calculated brutality, straight red card nowadays but just pale yellow in the era of 'bites your legs' Hunter or Storey or Droy. With Lewington levitating and the midfield unsettled, bottom of the table Fulham went on to beat top of the table Chelsea by three goals to one.

We were forgiven in March 1980. Ray wrote for Michael Heatley of his favourite seasons and the match of his life – November 1982: Wolves 2 Fulham 4. That was then in Division Two and this is now in the Premiership. Season

2007–08 can hardly have been a favourite one for Ray but as a coach his match of matches must be Fratton Park, 11th May 2008.

Looking back to 1987, Ray talks of a traumatic period during his first year of management – "one which I shall never forget nor wish on anyone." Ray explains: "It was at 5.27pm when the telephone rang at Craven Cottage. It was Mr Bulstrode. He told me he had just bought QPR and intended to merge Fulham with them at Loftus Road. Would I telephone the players and tell them as it would probably be on the TV and radio at 6pm. He did not mention that QPR already had a manager and a playing staff."

Anxious times indeed, and the main task was the fight to save the football club.

Ray talks about the Fulham fans: "You were marvellous. The only thing which gave the players and staff happiness then was the reaction of the Fulham supporters. It helped tremendously to know that you all really cared. We just had to soldier on, walking wounded and all."

So we did just that. We soldiered on, walking wounded and all. Fulham 2000 was founded. We soldiered on and we fought the good fight (against the best advice of Rodney Marsh, Paul Parker and David Mellor MP). Fulham's old soldiers walked on, walked on with hope in their hearts. Captain Beaky walked on and on to Brighton to raise funds for Fulham 2000. Fulham's 'Dad's Army' made it through to 1997. Promotion was gained and the ground was saved. Final score – Walking Wounded 2 Developers 0.

I have said before it but I must say it again. "Thanks Ray," and how appropriate that you should be leading the teams out as we celebrated our

return to Craven Cottage in July 2004. How splendid that you should be at the manager's right hand in the crisis of 2007–08. Lucky Roy and lucky us! Saving the club 1987, saving the team 2008. All in a day's work for Ray Lewington.

With his best French accent, Freddie Fulham says: "Vraiment formidable!"

Soldiering on. Chelsea pensioners show how to do it – but Fulham's pensioners do it better.

HAPPY DAYS

HAPPY DAYS are here again!

The good ship 'Friends of Fulham' sets sail in September 1995. Below: JT – a genius.

5pm, 11th May 2008. Mission accomplished.

BLUE IS THE COLOUR

SOME OF MY best friends support Chelsea. Some of my family support Chelsea. At Emanuel 1984–1994 most of my pupils supported Chelsea and the Harrodian years 1996–2008 have seen more and more pupils wearing Chelsea wristbands.

Oh, Chelsea! You are very successful for sure, but much of the time you're a miserable lot. Blue is the colour, your colour (and your disposition, humour, temperament); you're over-inclined to the moody blues! And what about your singing of the blues? You seem to sing in the soulful manner of a Bessie Smith.

We are only a poor little Fulham but we do love a cheery, gladsome sound.

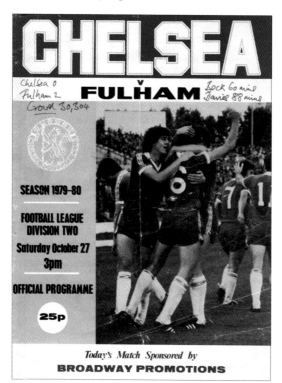

Today's Match Sponsored by
BROADWAY PROMOTIONS

Alan (Fulham's number one window cleaner) sings along with George Formby. Hugh Grant prefers Gene Kelly *Singing in the Rain* when watching Fulham lose 10–0 up at Liverpool.

On 11th May 2008 Setanta brought you 'High Noon'. High Noon at Fratton Park where Fulham won the shoot-out. Not pretty, but a win it was. All those Fulham fans who were low, very low, in April have been singing and dancing throughout May and well into July.

Meanwhile Chelsea's supporters are far from happy with all their silver medals. Fed up with jokes about the Barnsley chop, miserable in Moscow – they mutter over the might have beens of Wembley and the league. Never mind their wealth, their impeccable home record and their years of European football, it is Anelka this and Terry that as they dwell upon the unfairness of Russian roulette. Sack the manager, sack the manager!

What about FFC? Compare and contrast them with the special ones. FFC, less money, less talented players and less acceptable results. Often vulnerable at home and dismal away. Contrast Chelsea who are second in Europe and second in the Premiership. Congratulations!

Fulham spend 22 games in the relegation zone and finish with the same number of points as relegated Reading. A terrible season, the worst results in 14 years and yet their fans are grinning from ear to ear.

Freddie Fulham says: "Still Premier League, still having a larf!"

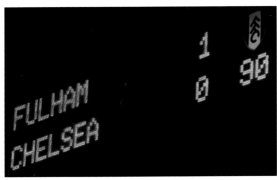

"Some of my best friends support Chelsea..." True blue Simon Parker wears a scarf of green, but is pure gold as a teacher at Harrodian. Right: a Chelsea wedding for Amanda Thomson.

COMMUNITY SERVICE

BACK IN 1951 it was all about national service and many a follower of the Fulham might expect to spend two years listening out for results while soldiering in Germany. Others might be in Cyprus with the RAF or on the high seas with the RN or the Royal Marines. Johnny Haynes was excused national service because of a dodgy ear.

Some were exempt from national service in the 1950s but no-one is exempt from community service nowadays. The Premiership years have seen a dramatic expansion in community projects at home and overseas. FFC has taken a lead in such work. Quite right too.

"You're in the army now!" Preparing for national service, July 1956 (author smoking pipe of peace).

Pioneering leadership was provided by Gary Mulcahey from 1995 to 2008.

'Help the Homestead' football tournament at Harrodian, September 2006. Guest of honour – Simon Morgan; winner of Rettie Cup for sportsmanship – Ryan Todd.

Gerald (in FFC kit) with his Homestead XI in September 2006. Michelle (in FFC kit) coaching Harrodians girls in September 2005.

Then Mr Fulham himself took over as head of community. Simon Morgan expanded Gary's work with such success that he was headhunted by the national coaches in 2006. Simon remains in touch with Fulham and was cheering the team on against Aston Villa in March 2008.

Simon also took a close interest in the Homestead hostels for street children, a community project sponsored by Fulham fans in Barnes to serve the homeless in Cape Town. Note the FFC badges worn by the football coach Gerald. Gerald is the main man in Cape Town and Michelle is the link between London and the Homestead. Formerly a member of the FFC community team, Michelle

taught at the Harrodian School before dedicating her time to pioneering projects in Africa.

Many Harrodians have become involved in community service on behalf of the Homestead. Chaz is depicted above aged 11 on his first visit to Cape Town and again aged 15 making music at a fund raising concert. Chaz has a younger brother, George (pictured below), who plays his football with FFC. The Downs Syndrome team often appear on the pitch at half-time for penalty shoot-outs and walkabouts.

The Whelton family support Fulham as season ticket holders (Riverside block T) but for them the community schemes mean that FFC is more, much more, than a Saturday club.

One more time, then, Fulham. Not so much a programme, more a way of life!

Community service – a family affair for the Wheltons.

HULL UNIVERSITY

LARKIN ABOUT IN HULL

PHILIP LARKIN WAS university librarian at Hull for 39 years. Images of Hull appear in his poem *Here*. "Here cranes cluster beside barge-crowded water… fishy smelling streets, the slave museum, tattoo shops, grim head-scarfed wives…"

Here in Larkinland I asked a far from grim head-scarfed wife the way to the KC stadium. We talked of the old ground at Boothferry Park and we discussed Billy Bremner. We remembered the relegations of those days and we celebrated the promotions of these days. Fishy smelling streets there were and chippy smelling fans there were, tattoo shops and betting shops there were, and many tiger-costumed fans there were larking about in Larkin Park on the way to their KC stadium. New ground for Fulham but not for Pete (the Diamond) Smith who saw me safely to my seat. We were soon engulfed in a vast red banner devised by Ormondroyd's crew who had taken the 7am train to collect their images of Larkinland. They were up for it and so was JP (our recruit from West Ham), blowing kisses and waving, waving.

So far so good, but I was worried. August and September fixtures against Hull seldom read well in the *Cottagers' Journals*. "Our lads had the early advantage but they failed to push that advantage home… Hull's Citizens were less efficient in many ways but they were nippy and keen and they played to win." Thus it was in the opening fixture of the 1907 season and thus it proved in the opening fixture in August 2008. Our lads had the early advantage and the early goal as Bullard crossed for the Korean to score with a well directed header. Out came the LG clappers – clap, clap, clap – but then "our lads failed to push that advantage home." Still passing well, still the better side but missing three clear chances. The Tigers were "less efficient in many ways but they were nippy and keen and played to win." Fulham larkin about, Tigers tigerish. Fulham lost in 1907 and Fulham lost in 2008.

Excellent cellarman at The Wellington before the match. Thank you, Mr Gant! Compassionate folk at The Hole in the Wall after the match where Summer Lightning beer was the obvious choice. Summer lightning can strike twice and it did – late summer 1907 and late summer 2008.

No more Larkin about in Hull. Home we go via Doncaster and Peterborough (memories, memories) and so to King's Cross where Steven and I part. Last word from Philip Larkin: "supine." Fulham's performance / underperformance in the second half was just that, "negligently inert," verily supine. Last word from Steven: "Great day out – pity about the football!"

From Ormondroyd's album – new season, new ground.

A CENTURY OF TIGERS

THE TIGERS of 1908, as depicted in that year by Henri Rousseau – "burning bright in the forests" for this knight of jungle art. An illustration that would have added lustre to the Merula account of our match with Hull.

In front of those tigers in the picture must be the Manchester City playmakers. Note their agility and cavalier style. It suited Fulham in the FA Cup match in February 1908 when we won 3–1 (as it did in April 2008 when we exploited their relaxed approach to convert 0–2 into 3–2). Let us hope for more such entertainment in early December when they visit Craven Cottage in the Premiership.

As for the tigers of Hull – we won the return fixture in 1908 and we must do so in March 2009.

WHAT A DIFFERENCE A WEEK MAKES
or "A LIFE IN THE DAY OF..."

A Life in the Day

AUGUST 23rd 2008. In the *Sunday Times* feature the contributors always seem to discuss their breakfast rituals. Let's skip breakfast and the joys of the allotment at 0800hrs, 1100hrs shopping in Sloane Square and high noon cycling past a deserted Stamford Bridge. Fast forward to the main event this Saturday: Fulham v Arsenal.

Late kick off (5.30pm) for the benefit of Setanta, but some followers of the Fulham still reach Craven Cottage at the usual time of 2.00pm. I have an early appointment at the Fulham ticket office in order to return Sandra's precious photograph of Mary Doughty. Conversation turns to the Haynes statue. Sandra confirms progress and, of course, the willingness of Barbara B to lead the Friends of Fulham on a bucket collection in aid of the statue fund. (Sure enough, Barbara is in action at the Hammersmith End this very day.)

Dress code as pictured here, hence some confusion when I met this loyal supporter (below). She seemed to think I was Geoffrey Boycott working for Setanta. Understandable perhaps, given the profusion of TV crews at the Hammersmith End. Further confusion when one of these crews requested my

comments on Fulham's prospects for the new season. Somehow this interview to camera turned into an extended discussion of football in Croatia. The cameraman and his wife had filmed in Split and Zagreb. The Torcida Ultra were known to them. I promised to send my new best friends a copy of *Following the Fulham into Europe*. They promptly booked me for a studio interview before the Bolton match. If you want to get ahead get a hat?

Setanta covered our trip to Fratton Park in May 2008. Is that a favourable omen? Is the curse of Sky to be exchanged for the blessings of Setanta?

Cycle back to SW14 to rescue yet more precious photos from the Mortlake sorting office – an Intertoto album containing rare footage from Finland, Sochaux and Berlin. Cycle to the Cottage via Becky and Derek at The Bricklayer's Arms. Derek examines the Intertoto album and kindly identifies some of the Hamburg based Fulham fans.

4.55pm and time to move off to Toofif corner where David Lloyd is busy, busy, but Ken Coton has time to take possession of the Intertoto album. Some animated discussion of just which image from Finland is most Fulhamish.

5.20pm and seated. Seated as usual with Jeremy Fordham, but this afternoon we are not joined by Piers Butler. His place has gone to Tokai Jim over from Cape Town – a most enthusiastic addition to the Riverside mutes. Where, I wonder, is his Gooner of a father-in-law this afternoon?

5.25pm. Enough idle banter and over to David Hamilton for his "Show time!" LG clappers at the ready, we are in good voice and determined to lift the team. Behold another flying start from Fulham and another well worked set piece from Jimmy Bullard which is converted this time by Hangeland.

After the first stylish 20 minutes up at Hull we faded and we were especially disappointing in midfield. Not so this afternoon. Murphy is on fire and passing well. The Arsenal are rattled and are not passing well. "Supine Gunners – what's the score?"

6.30pm. Leaning on the wall at half-time admiring the river scene but agonising over our inability to defend a one-goal lead. Back to the seats and back to business. Tokai Jim's clapper is starting to fall apart but the Fulham back four do not shred under pressure.

It is the 70th minute and Roy Hodgson notices signs of panic. Fulham are tiring and the Arsenal have more and more of the ball. What if they equalise? Will we yet again collapse in the final minutes? No? No? No! Despite a flurry of Arsenal free kicks and corners the Fulham back four hold out and Schwarzer is strong. (Stronger than Warner last August.) Mr Atkinson stretches his three extra minutes into four or five but this Arsenal lack the finesse of yesteryear. We hold out. We win 1–0.

Not quite as distinguished a performance as in November 2006 but still jolly good and just what we needed after stumbling at Hull.

7.55pm. Tokai Jim and Jeremy are all smiles as I leave them and head off to the Hammersmith End for a word with Ormondroyd and Derek. A quick word and a "See you here on Wednesday for the Leicester game!"

Now for a leisurely cycle ride to Hammersmith Bridge. A nod and a smile from Dennis Turner as he gets into his car. Cycling past the Crabtree I meet up with Nick Wood and young Matthew. Onwards to the Riverside Studios where I catch up with Nick's brother Charles (a veteran goalkeeper who approves of Schwarzer); then, almost inevitably as we have overcome the Gooners, along comes Hugh Fordham to report on a glowing Thames. Aglow, aglow indeed.

The best remark of all is from Daniel Fordham (aged 5) following his very first visit to Craven Cottage: "Fulham beated Arsenal!"

Yes, beated and well beated.

The *Sunday Times* contributors usually itemise the evening meal before their particular Saturday night fever. Beans from the allotment, raspberries from the allotment, then study the football results as collated by Sheila. She sets the video recorder for *Match of the Day* as I nod off with that grateful grin which betokens happy daze, happy doze.

Nick Wood and young Matthew.

ULHAM, ULHAM, WHAT'S THE SCORE?

WHEN FULHAM BEAT Birmingham in April 1975 a remarkable number of long-lost friends rang in to enquire about cup final tickets. They hadn't been to Craven Cottage for years but they had always supported Fulham. They soon drifted away again after Wembley. Same story in 1981–82 and 1982–83 as Super Mac's team seemed to be heading for a promotion double. Bandwagon boys and girls have we.

David Mellor MP was just such a Fulham fan for a couple of seasons but as the going got tough for the Ulham he relocated to Stamford Bridge. I asked for his help with the campaign to save Craven Cottage and received this reply.

Paul Parker and Rodney Marsh

> **THE RT HON DAVID MELLOR** QC MP
>
> Member of Parliament for
> Putney
>
> *[signature]*
> Thank you very much for your letter about Fulham.
>
> Sadly there is nothing I would like more than for Fulham to stay on at Craven Cottage. I fear the dice are inevitably loaded against them because there isn't the same pressure for the Club to stay as there was with Chelsea, and the Craven Cottage site, being on the river, is so much more attractive for re-development. But certainly, I shall not want to be anything other than constructive on this, and am ready to help out in any way that might be useful.

took the same line. Craven Cottage was doomed. The brave new world was at Loftus Road. Fulham Park Rangers as the Man Utd of the south? You know it makes sense!

Ulham are not interested in sense and sensibility. Ulham may have lost an F or two (for years the Riverside Stand sign sent out just that message – ULHAM FOOTBALL CLUB). We waited ten years for the sign to be corrected, by which time Ulham the team had dropped a division or two. Ulham were beaten 10–0 by Liverpool, then they were fully stretched by Kingstonian and by Bath, and finally they were seen off by non-leaguers such as Hayes and Yeovil. Worse than the Yeovil in 1993 and worse than 92nd-placed Torquay in 1996. Only the lonely were obdurate enough to stick by Ulham.

Tokai Jim often talks of that epic evening when two or three were gathered together at the Hammersmith End for FFC 1 Scunthorpe 3. Well worth the flight from sunny Cape Town to shiver along with 2,175 others that January in 1996. The hangman from the Evening Standard made mighty mock but *Toofif* answered with a classic cover – *We Can Still Make the Play-offs*. Lloyd's XI v Hangman's XI was a home win. Home, sweet home itself was at risk. League status was at risk and soon we are losing 2–0 to non-league Ashford.

Are we downhearted? No, we're singing in the rain. The Ulham may appear to be drowning but really we are waving. We are waving and we are cheering. Cheering not jeering because we have heard those words: "Keep the faith!" Micky Adams himself is out there in the wind and the rain – practising what he preached. Walking on water and waltzing on water as he put away a couple of penalties. 2–2 and we all floated back to Craven Cottage. It would have been sensible to exit Ashford in the London direction but the Ulham don't do sensible, so instead our driver headed off towards the Channel Tunnel.

Cue for a song. How about "This year we're going to win the Cup! Sing viva el Fulham!" No, no – why state the obvious? The Ulham don't do the obvious just as they don't do the sensible. The Ulham keep the faith and the Ulham dream dreams. As one they rise and sing: "Ulham into Europe, Ulham into Europe!" This may seem to be a tall story but it is a true story. I can call a lawyer (Professor Roodyn) and a chef (Josef) as expert witnesses. "Ulham into Europe!" Close your eyes and fast forward a manager or three. Open your eyes and behold there we are in Bologna winning the Interoto Cup. "Score Inamoto, we're going to score in a moto!" and score we did.

I made jolly sure that I went to the Sochaux match via Ashford. It may have taken 19 hours but it was worth every minute to revisit such a turning point in the unofficial history of the Ulham. In Churchillspeak – it may not have been the beginning of the end but assuredly it was the end of the beginning. Our very own El Alamain? Bernard Law Montgomery Adams did not lead us out at Loftus Road when we actually won the gold cup (cuplet) but he set us on the way. As, of course, did Jimmy Hill and the Muddymans, the Shrimptons and Cyril Swain.

Who is that I see in Zagreb? David Shrimpton and son. What is it that I spy with my little eye? What is it that Sheila catches with her little camera? It is the official scoreboard with the official score. DINAMO 0 ULHAM 3.

UEFA Cup glory for the Ulham but not for those sensible souls Mellor, Marsh and Parker. Only The Lonely XI v The Doubting Thomas XI. Another improbable scoreline – 3–0 to Only The Lonely.

DUE NORTH? DUE SOUTH?

30th AUGUST 2008. The last Saturday of the school holidays and the last chance for some sun and sand ahead of the long, long autumn term. Obviously we must head due south to Sussex. Sussex by the sea.

On the other hand we could follow the Fulham due north to Old Trafford for another entertaining encounter with VDS and Saha's last but one club. Due north? Due south? Decisions, decisions – which not for the first time in the Premiership are taken for us by the tyros of TV. Manchester United are required

in Moscow so FFC must await the schedules and reschedules to be announced some time sooner or later, probably later. Thus not due north with FFC but due south with Sheila. Due South indeed for sea food beside the sea.

After the fine food and fine wine it is time for a walk along the sea front to Hove and then back via the Lanes to the Seagull

Centre. Here the fans of Brighton and Hove Albion can browse through old programmes or purchase the new blue replica kit. I asked for a photo of Zamora but all were long gone/sold out. There were some copies of Mullers' memoirs but these I resisted, and invested instead in a ticket for Saturday's match with Leyton Orient.

A delightful Scotsman from the Celtic half of Glasgow sold me my ticket once we had listened to a senior Seagull's polemic on the Premiership. Mr Seagull was very happy not to be involved in "the boring, boring, ever so predictable march of the wealthy Chelsea. How dare they call themselves the Blues when they are really just Russian gold? Hooray for the lower leagues where any team can beat any team and real supporters can have their say."

Having had his say, he moved off to repeat himself at the souvenir stand and I got a chance to choose my seat. The Celtic fan at the ticket desk advised as shown here, so off I went back to the sea and the sun. Sheila was not surprised (though underwhelmed) by plans for the morrow but the weather was set fair to very fair so she anticipated a couple of hours of reading and writing undisturbed by PFT. Sheila has her own memories of cold, cold afternoons at the Goldstone. An 0–0 attritional encounter or two, plus a League Cup romp in August 1995 when we won there (5–0 on aggregate). Those were the days when we thought that Michael Mison might be the answer. He wasn't but Conroy scored twice in that fixture and eventually he did develop into the answer and more than the answer – "Super, super Mick, super Micky Conroy!" and "Conroy from the half-way line, Conroy from the half-way line."

But this was the Withdean Stadium. Nothing particularly super about the Withdean. A touch of the Twertons in its inaccessibility and a dash of Bologna in the athletics track surrounding the pitch. Worse than the antiquated Fratton Park for exposing visitors to wind and rain but quite unlike Pompey for chimers and chimes. Most unlike the Goldstone for choir power. Mute to the point of eerie for much of this match.

Nothing on offer from the 200+ Orient supporters and not much more from the senior Seagulls around me. Some chat about the difficulties of parking and how much worse it would all be for the forthcoming League Cup fixture with Man City. The first half drifted away without structure or incident. Weather 10/10. Football 2/10.

For the second half I moved off to the family enclosure, which was better for sunbathing. Again precious little banter and just the occasional "Seagulls, Seagulls." Two early attacks on the Orient goal woke some of the fans but, despite generous numbers of water stops, the players soon wilted into ineptitude. I decided to slip away before the final whistle in order to catch a 4.51pm bus to the sea front. An ancient Seagull was there before me. He remembered Morgs, he remembered Zamora, he remembered Peter Ward and "Smith must score" at Wembley. He rated that Peter O'Sullivan who went to Fulham and that Teddy Maybank who came from Fulham. Yes, he missed the Goldstone, he really missed the Goldstone.

5.22pm. Back on the beach enjoying the evening sunshine. Was it good to be away from the Premiership? Was it fun back where we were for 33 years, back in our natural bread and butter surroundings, our fish and chip surroundings. Yes – if all you want is a quiet afternoon. The football was uninspired and uninspiring. The ground was quaint and the company bland. The major plus was the charming stewarding – all smiles and courtesy.

Brighton v Orient ought to have been Us v Them, Sussex v The Smoke, up and at 'em! It had been that and more when Millwall took their thousands to the Goldstone (police helicopters by the dozen and sirens, sirens throughout the afternoon). The total lack of atmosphere this August was almost as disappointing as the poverty of the football. I don't suppose FFC were all that talented a team in 1996–97 when we last met the Seagulls in the league but I do recall plenty of badinage and bravado down at the Goldstone. A no-score draw but not a no-score bore.

This August's Brighton 0 Orient 0 was that real deal – a no-score, many-a-snore draw. Wonderful weather, pity about the football – must get back to the beach.

Without Conroy (who struck again in the home win over Brighton in 1997), without Adams and Morgs – we might still be bumbling about at the Withdean. Promotion helped to market the club and the buyer promised us the Premiership within five years. We didn't really believe him but gosh how we enjoyed the ride! 1999 was good and 2001 was better. RLS of Edinburgh warned us that it is better to travel hopefully than to arrive. Under JT that season of seasons we travelled (how we travelled) and assuredly we arrived. We arrived in the Premiership (in only four years...) and we survived in the Premiership.

Not always easy and often not jolly, but whenever I have exploited opportunities to sample some lower league football (Boston, Brighton, Cambridge, Exeter, Hearts, Livingston, Southend, Torquay) I have come away reconciled to the Premiership.

Due north is fine for pre-season, due south is fun in the sun, but Premiership football at the refurbished Craven Cottage is generally watchable and occasionally enthralling. We walk away at our peril. It's not "just as good on TV." Sorry, armchair fans Alan and Robert – "It's *not* just as good on TV."

Back to Boston, Cambridge, Exeter, Hearts, Livingston, Southend, Torquay and Withdean – that life in the lower leagues which is our natural constituency. Indeed it once was and indeed it might be so again; but for the moment give thanks to Chairman Mo and make the very most of our time at the top table. Talk to friends at Reading and Derby about their new life or lack of life in the Championship. They are miserable away from the big time buzz.

So, come on, you whites – face the facts. Last season you won the best behaved spectators award, this season you might target the Fair Play league while quietly dignifying the lower end of the top table. At the elite end of this top table it is more and more like the Mad Hatter's tea party. Billionaires are replaced by zillionaires at Man City (who promptly lose to Brighton...). Absurd sums are offered for any and every superstar. Managers are out after three matches at Newcastle and West Ham. Mayhem and meltdown all around while down by the riverside we quietly press on with the Haynes statue. Artists off the field working away to honour the artist of artists on the field – the finest

footballer ever to play for Fulham.

Johnny Haynes was content to spend his entire career at Craven Cottage. Captain of Fulham, captain of England, diplomat of distinction, a modest genius, a gentleman and a gentle man. If with a little help from Old Fulham and a lot of help from George Cohen we can uphold the spirit of 1966 then the Premiership will benefit from our presence. We have the most beautiful ground in the league; let us under Roy Hodgson and Ray Lewington stand for the good old ways and the good old days. After a week or two in the footballing wilderness (Brighton 30th August and then on to Cambridge 6th September where the chairman, Phil Law, had resigned following fan rant and rage) I return to Mortlake enlightened – yes, a wiser man.

At Brighton and Cambridge they are sadly not Arcadians, nor even are they Corinthians playing for the fun and the joy of the beautiful game. Due south are the sleeping dogs of Brighton and Hove Albion while due north are the pale blue rant/ragers of Cambridge – take your pick. Let's not sink down there again. Let us instead cultivate the Premiership garden. We are not the Man Utd of the south, we are not the Man City of the south, we are not the Chelsea of SW6 – no, we are the Cottagers, modest market gardeners of the London league. Look due north, look due south and then give thanks this 17th of October. It is the Maestro's birthday. It falls on a Friday this year and on Saturday 18th October we are at home to Sunderland.

First however we were at home to Bolton. Thus on September 13th it was Cottagers v Trotters, it was Hodgson and Lewington v Megson. It was Haynes v Lofthouse. All a bit 1950ish? All a bit Tommy Trinderish? All a bit "Oh, you lucky people"-ish? Yes, assuredly, modestly, muddlingly, mumblingly, mellifluously yes. We are the luckiest of lucky people. Let us give most humble and hearty thanks down by the riverside.

AND SO TO BED

"AND SO TO bed..." The words come from the diary of a Cambridge man (1651–54) and a Pauline (1646–50) – an expert on dockyards.

The writing of Samuel Pepys in the 1660s is still an inspiration to diarists in general and this diarist in particular. I was, like Pepys, a Cambridge man (1957–61) and a Pauline (1961–1984). Many Cambridge friends appear in the

pages of this diary and several Paulines have kindly contributed comments and photographs. Like Pepys, I have visited many dock-yards and I rejoice that Pepys preserved this version of the Mary Rose in his library. For the real thing you must go to Portsmouth. We did on the 11th of May 2008.

AND SO TO BED

A Cambridge bed (a right royal Victoria and Albert bed) but not the bed of Samuel Pepys.

It is a bed that I know well. I used it first in 1961 and it is a bed to which Sheila and I have retired after some deeply depressing visits to the Abbey

Stadium. In December 1979 there was a close encounter with Ernie Clay at the Great Gate of Trinity College. "We always win here and we will win with ease this afternoon!" Chairmanspeak followed by a comfortable win – a com-fortable win for Cambridge. 4–0.

How appropriate that we were back in Cambridge to celebrate promotion in May 1997 finally achieving that long awaited 'comfortable win'. The Premiership years have not involved the Abbey Stadium but the Fulham family have extended their CAMRA researches at The Cambridge Blue. The Thomson family have visited and revisited the Pepys diary at Magdalene College and have rested on the royal bed at Trinity. What better way to celebrate a Premiership victory?

In January 2004 it was Fulham 2 Everton 1, with goals from Saha and Steed. A most timely win at Loftus Road then off to Cambridge for a bit of a dinner. Flowers for the golden girl in black and white.

And so to bed.

Flowers for the golden girl in black and white.

www.ashwaterpress.co.uk